ADVANCED LEVEL ECONOMICS

Data
Response

ADVANCED LEVEL ECONOMICS

Data Response

ANDY McCANN
and
SAMMY WILSON

JOHN MURRAY

© Andy McCann & Sammy Wilson 1995

First published in 1995
by John Murray (Publishers) Ltd
50 Albemarle Street, London W1X 4BD

Reprinted 1996, 1997

Layout by Eric Drewery
Cover design by John Townson/Creation
Typeset by Servis Filmsetting Ltd, Manchester
Printed and bound in Great Britain by The University Press, Cambridge

A CIP catalogue entry for this title can be obtained from the British Library.

ISBN 0 7195 7019 0 Student's Book
ISBN 0 7195 7010 7 Teacher's Pack (Student's Book plus Model Answers)

Contents

Acknowledgements   vi

Introduction   vii

1 *Skills and techniques*   1

What is data?   3
Analysing the data   5
Exercises   20

2 *Common themes in data response questions*   25

Inflation   27
Unemployment   33
The balance of payments   39
Exchange rates   47
Public finance   52
Market failure   67

3 *Data response questions*   73

Approaching the question   75
Market system v. planned system   *Questions 1–2*   79
Demand and supply   *Questions 3–7*   82
Industrial economics   *Questions 8–11*   88
The macro-economic state of the economy   *Questions 12–18*   94
Unemployment   *Questions 19–20*   105
Inflation   *Questions 21–23*   108
International trade and exchange rates   *Questions 24–30*   112
Tax and government spending   *Questions 31–36*   122
The European Union   *Questions 37–40*   132
Population   *Questions 41–42*   138

Answers to the exercises   **141**

Index   **149**

Acknowledgements

The authors and publishers are grateful to the following for permission to use copyright material.

The Associated Examining Board, pp. 19 and 71–2
Barclays Bank, pp. 100–1
Belfast News Letter/Century Newspapers Ltd, p. 108
Central Statistical Office, p. 102 from London Business School of Econometric Model, pp. 124 and 126 from the Family Expenditure Survey
© The Telegraph plc, London, 1994, p. 109
The Financial Times, pp. 37–8, 51, 70, 79, 84, 96, 99, 103, 119 and 121
HMSO, pp. 60, 92–3, 124 and 138 from *Social Trends*, p. 107 from *Regional Trends*
The *Independent*/Newspaper Publishing plc, p. 132
Lloyds Bank, pp. 98, 114, 117 and 122
The *Mail on Sunday*/Solo Syndication & Literary Agency Ltd, p. 91, © The *Mail on Sunday*/Solo
National Westminster Bank, p. 71–2
The Northern Ireland Economic Council, pp. 134 and 136, reproduced by permission of the Northern Ireland Economic Council
Northern Ireland Council for the Curriculum, Examinations and Assessment (NICCEA, formerly NISEAC), pp. 10–12, 37–8, 65–6, 86–7, 92–3, 100–1 and 128–9; NICCEA bears no responsibility for the model answers to questions taken from its past question papers which are included in the Model Answers section of this publication
The Royal Bank of Scotland, p. 80, reproduced by kind permission of The Royal Bank of Scotland plc from The Royal Bank of Scotland Review No. 172, December 1991. Article entitled 'The Priceless Countryside: The Recreational Benefits of Environmental Goods'. Author, Dr K.G. Willis; and p. 116 reproduced by kind permission of The Royal Bank of Scotland Review No. 171, September 1991. Article entitled 'British Merchant Shipping: Market Forces and the Defence of the Realm'. Author, Dr Michael Asteris
The Scottish Examination Board, pp. 32–3
Times Newspapers Ltd, p. 85 *The Times*, London © Times Newspapers Ltd 1993/94, pp. 65–6, 86, 88, 105, 111, 112, 130 and 133 *The Sunday Times*, London © Times Newspapers Ltd 1993/94
University of Cambridge Local Examinations Syndicate (UCLES), pp. 15 and 45–6, reproduced by permission of the University of Cambridge Local Examinations Syndicate
University of London Examinations and Assessment Council (ULEAC), pp. 51 and 70

Every effort has been made to contact copyright holders. The publishers apologise for any omissions and will be pleased to correct this at the earliest opportunity.

Introduction

There is no escape! If you want to study A level Economics then you will have to face a data response paper.

For some students this is a daunting prospect. It is the paper in which otherwise competent candidates are most likely to underperform. The reason for this is that revision and preparation are very difficult to organise.

Data response questions are not primarily a test of knowledge, and so rote learning from your notes is unlikely to be of much benefit. They test a range of analytical skills and may require you to apply economic theories in a variety of practical but often unfamiliar contexts. For instance, you are not likely to be asked to describe how markets operate but you might be asked to analyse a free market solution to the problem of, say, traffic congestion. In short, data response questions are a very demanding form of assessment.

This book aims to provide you not only with the skills required to answer data response questions but also with some background to the contemporary economic issues on which data response questions are frequently based.

Chapter 1

Skills and techniques

What is data?

Data simply means information, and a data response question is one that is based upon information given to you by the examiner.

Much of the material needed for your answer will be given to you in the question and the examination will, in part, be a test of your ability to understand, reorganise, analyse and present this information.

Do not make the mistake, however, of assuming that a data response paper requires no prior knowledge of economics! In fact, the examiner will very often be using the data as stimulus material specifically to assess your economic knowledge and competence.

I THOUGHT YOU DIDN'T NEED TO KNOW **ANYTHING** ABOUT **ECONOMICS** TO ANSWER A DATA RESPONSE QUESTION.

PRESENTATION OF DATA

There are three basic formats in which data can be presented to you:

- **the written word**: many questions are based on newspaper and magazine articles or extracts from government publications
- **tables**: numerical information is often given in the form of tables, etc.
- **charts and diagrams**: bar charts, pie diagrams and time-series graphs are frequently used in data response questions.

In practice most examinations use data presented in more than one format.

SOURCES OF DATA

Government publications are the most important source of information on the performance of the economy and examiners make frequent use of official statistics in compiling data response questions. The most important government publications, all published by HMSO, are listed below.

- *The United Kingdom National Accounts*, better known as the **Blue Book**, deals with national income statistics. It is published in September each year and covers all aspects of the UK economy, giving details for the previous 11 years.
- *The United Kingdom Balance of Payments*, better known as the **Pink Book**, gives details of all UK transactions with the rest of the world, with data going back for 11 years.
- *The Financial Statement and Budget Report*, better known as the **Red Book**, is published at the time of the Budget and outlines the proposed tax changes and public expenditure plans for the year ahead. It also contains the government's frequently inaccurate economic forecasts.
- ***Social Trends*** describes how we live and spend our money. It contains a wealth of detail on issues as diverse as church attendance, hobbies, income and health. It is an invaluable snapshot of life in contemporary Britain.

- *Regional Trends* provides data on which comparisons can be made between the various regions of the UK. It deals with topics such as population, education, health, income and spending.
- *Economic Trends* is a compilation of all the main economic indicators, and is liberally illustrated with charts and diagrams.
- The *Annual Abstract of Statistics* is a must for economists, as it contains information from most of the above publications in a single volume. It is obviously cheaper to buy one *Annual Abstract of Statistics* than separate copies of the Pink Book, the Blue Book, *Regional Trends*, etc.

There are also many useful non-governmental sources of data such as:

- the economic reviews published by the major banking groups
- articles in 'quality' newspapers and magazines such as *The Economist*, *The Financial Times*, *The Times*, the *Guardian* and many others
- the financial pages of teletext.

Some questions in A level data response papers are based on information taken from more than one source and in a few cases no source is given. Listed below are some of the sources used in recent data response questions from various examination boards.

- the 1987 Annual Report of the National Food Survey Committee
- *Economic Trends*, 1988
- the 1988 Blue Book
- the HMSO *Financial Statement and Budget Report*, 1989/90
- a government consultation document entitled 'Summer Time' dealing with the economic and social implications of a change in the UK time zone
- the UK Family Expenditure Survey
- *Social Trends*, 1992
- Barclay's Bank Economic Review
- *The Sunday Times*
- *The Economist*
- *Economic Trends*, 1992
- *OECD Financial Statistics*, 1992
- the *Independent*
- *The Financial Times*

Clearly there is a predominance of government publications and you would be well advised to spend some time familiarising yourself with their content and layout.

Analysing the data

This is not an examination in statistics and you will not be expected to calculate standard deviations, correlation coefficients or any other statistical mumbo jumbo. However, you will be expected to show an understanding of some simple statistical concepts and techniques.

This section is designed to familiarise you with the techniques involved in calculating and using:

- percentages
- index numbers
- averages (including weighted averages such as the retail price index and the sterling trade index)
- real and money values
- seasonally adjusted data
- relationships between variables.

PERCENTAGES

Calculating percentages might seem a fairly elementary skill and so indeed it is. However, a surprisingly large number of candidates lose marks every year by making basic errors in their calculations.

Calculating the percentage change

Suppose the price of shares in a fictitious company, Eureka Holdings plc, were to move as follows:

Date	Price	% change
1 January	£2.00	
2 January	£2.50	
3 January	£3.00	
4 January	£4.00	
5 January	£3.00	

The method of calculating the percentage change is quite simple.

1 Deduct the original figure from the next figure.
2 Divide this difference by the original figure.
3 Multiply by 100.

So when the share price rises from £2.00 to £2.50 the percentage change is

$$\frac{£0.50}{£2.00} \times 100 = 25\%$$

The completed table will look like this:

Date	Price	% change
1 January	£2.00	—
2 January	£2.50	25
3 January	£3.00	20
4 January	£4.00	33.3
5 January	£3.00	-25

Confusion may arise when prices rise and fall. When the price rises from £3.00 to £4.00 the percentage rise is 33.3 per cent, but when the price falls from £4.00 to £3.00 the fall is only 25 per cent. It is the same absolute change but a different percentage.

Similarly, when a retailer buys stock at £2.00 per unit and sells it at £2.50 the mark-up is 25 per cent but the profit margin on his or her sales is only 20 per cent. The 50 pence profit is 25 per cent of what the retailer paid for the stock but only 20 per cent of the price at which it was sold.

Calculating the rate of inflation

Even more confusion may arise when data is presented in **index number** form. Consider the following figures for the retail price index (RPI):

Year	RPI	Inflation (%)
1985	100	
1986	104.8	
1987	109.2	
1988	115.1	
1989	117.6	

How do we calculate the rate of inflation, which is defined as the percentage increase in the retail price index over a period of one year?

Between 1986 and 1987 the index rose by 4.4 from 104.8 to 109.2. However, this is not the rate of inflation as 4.4 is only 4.2 per cent of the 1986 figure. It is important to remember that the absolute change in the RPI is the percentage change on the *base year* figure (in this case the 1985 figure), whereas the year-on-year inflation rate must be the change in the RPI as a percentage of the *previous year*'s RPI figure.

So the method of calculation for the rate of inflation for a particular year is as follows.

1 Find the change in the RPI between that year and the previous year.
2 Divide this figure by the RPI figure for the previous year.
3 Multiply by 100.

Thus the rate of inflation for 1988 is

$$115.1 - 109.2 = 5.9$$
$$\frac{5.9}{109.2} = 0.054$$
$$0.054 \times 100 = 5.4\%$$

The completed table will therefore look like this:

Year	RPI	Inflation (%)
1985	100	–
1986	104.8	4.8
1987	109.2	4.2
1988	115.1	5.4
1989	117.6	2.2

INDEX NUMBERS

This simple device enables users of data to see, at a glance, the percentage change on some previous year without the need for any calculations. The year against which such comparisons are made is known as the **base year** and is always given a value of 100.

Consider the following data on beer consumption.

Year	Beer consumption (£m)
1988	10 039
1989	10 676
1990	11 701
1991	12 849
1992	13 267

The construction of a 'beer consumption index', with 1988 as the base year, makes the above data much more user-friendly.

Year	Beer consumption index
1988	100
1989	106
1990	117
1991	128
1992	132

The casual reader with no desire for any cumbersome arithmetic can see immediately that beer sales rose by 6 per cent between 1988 and 1989 and by 32 per cent over the entire period.

This method of presentation is used extensively in government statistics. The following table is an example.

Year	National income (£m)	Index
1988	410 838	98
1989	420 005	100.2
1990 (base)	419 316	100
1991	405 397	96.7
1992	407 899	97.3

Again, the casual user of the figures can easily see the annual percentage change in national income and hence determine the rate of economic growth. The impact of the recession in the early 1990s is quite apparent.

Converting data into index number form

The conversion of raw data into index number form is a relatively simple calculation. It is carried out as follows:

$$\frac{\text{new figure}}{\text{base year figure}} \times 100$$

Hence the 1992 UK national income, expressed in index number form with 1990 as the base year, is

$$\frac{407\,899}{419\,316} \times 100$$

$$= 97.277 \text{ or simply } 97.3$$

Note that the same base year cannot be used for ever, and in the case of national income figures it is changed every five years. The base year currently in use is 1995; prior to this it was 1990.

Index numbers frequently appear in data response questions, with the retail price index being a particular favourite.

AVERAGES

Most students will be familiar with the idea of calculating the average of a set of numbers in order that we can use this figure as a guide to the larger group. The most common example of this is the **simple average**, otherwise known as the **arithmetic mean**.

Calculating the simple average

Suppose there are 11 students in a class and their marks in a recent test were 0, 5, 5, 15, 20, 25, 40, 40, 40, 55 and 60. To obtain the class average we simply add up the marks and divide the total by the number of students, giving us $\frac{305}{11}$ or 27.73.

Calculating the median and the mode

Another way in which the performance of this group of students could be represented by one figure would be to calculate the **median**.

This is the mark which exactly divides the class into two equal groups. In this case the median is 25, giving us five students below it (marks 0, 5, 5, 15 and 20) and five above it (marks 40, 40, 40, 55 and 60).

Finally, the class could be represented by the **mode**. The mode is the most frequently occurring mark, which in our example is 40.

WEIGHTED AVERAGES

In determining the simple average in the above example we treated all students' marks as being of equal importance. We simply totalled all the marks and divided by the number of students. However, there will be occasions when we wish to attach more importance to some of the figures than to others.

Consider the following question from an A level data response paper.

Average weekly income per household, UK, 1987/88	
Country	**Average income**
England	£277.80
Wales	£227.50
Scotland	£234.20
Ulster	£224.80
Entire UK	£270.00

Why is the average weekly household income in the UK (£270.00) not a simple average of the four figures given for England, Wales, Scotland and Ulster?

The simple average would be

$$\frac{277.8 + 227.5 + 234.2 + 224}{4}$$
$$= £241$$

The answer is that England has many more households than any of the other three countries and so should have a greater importance in the calculation of the overall UK average. This can be achieved by attaching to each country a weight that reflects its percentage of the total UK population.

Country	Average income	Weight (W)	W × average income
England	£277.80	83	23 057.4
Wales	£227.50	4	910.0
Scotland	£234.20	10	2 342.0
Ulster	£224.80	3	674.4
		Total 100	Total 26 983.8

$$\text{weighted average} = \frac{26\,983.8}{100} = 270$$

i.e. the total is divided by the sum of the weights, in this case 100.

The retail price index
The most common example of a weighted average in economics is the **retail price index (RPI)**. This is an attempt to represent in one figure the average change in the cost of living of the typical UK family. Hence it must attempt to measure the average change in the price of a whole basket of items.

Clearly some items in the expenditure of the normal family are more important than others. Housing, for example, should receive a higher weighting than fares and travel, as most families spend a higher proportion of their expenditure on it. The weights allocated to each item reflect the percentage of total spending it receives.

There are 14 broad groups of goods and services in the basic retail price index, with the sum of the weights coming to 1000. The groups are as follows.

Category	Weight (January 1992)
Food	151
Catering	47
Alcoholic drink	77
Tobacco	32
Housing	192
Fuel and light	46
Household goods	70
Household services	45
Clothing and footwear	63
Personal goods and services	38
Motoring	141
Fares and travel	20
Leisure goods	48
Leisure services	30
All items	1000

From this we can see that in 1992 the average family spent 15.1 per cent of total expenditure on food, 7.7 per cent on alcoholic drink, and so on.

This information is based on the Family Expenditure Survey. It is updated every year to take account of changing expenditure patterns and the development of new products such as satellite television.

Calculating changes in the RPI

You may be required to calculate changes in the RPI. Consider the following question from an A level multiple choice paper.

In calculating a retail price index, all goods and services are placed in one of the three categories in the table below.

Item	Weight	Current prices (base year = 100)
Food	5	110
Clothing	3	120
Others	2	130

What is the current value of the retail price index?

a 120   **b** 119   **c** 117   **d** 115   **e** 114

To arrive at the correct answer you need to:

1 multiply the current price index by the weight for each item
2 total these figures
3 divide this figure by the total of the weights.

Food	550
Clothing	360
Others	260
Total	1170

The sum of the weights is 10, and so the new figure for the RPI is

$$\frac{1170}{10} = 117$$

or option **c**.

The following question taken from a NICCEA A level paper tests your understanding of what the RPI represents and how it is constructed.

At its simplest level, the UK Index of Retail Prices is a weighted average of the price indices for fourteen broad groups of goods and services purchased by households in the UK.

The price indices relate the average price of goods in that group in a particular month to their average price at an earlier base date. The price indices are all given a value of 100 at the base date, so if, for example, in some month the price index for food were 200, it would indicate that on average food prices had doubled since the base date.

The weights (which are updated each year) reflect the relative importance of consumer spending on that broad group in total consumer spending. By construction the weights sum to 1,000 and so, for example, a weight of 200 for the food group would indicate that consumers devote about 20% of their total expenditure to foodstuffs.

At present, the Index of Retail Prices uses a base date of January 1987, whilst prior to 1987, the base date was January 1974. This question, which uses the data in the table below, compares the increase in retail prices over the five year period January 1974—January 1979, with the increase over the five year period January 1987—January 1992. Information is also provided on the weights used in calculating the January 1979 index, and those used in calculating the January 1992 index.

Category of Good or Service	Price Index January 1979 (Jan. 1974 = 100)	Weight used in January 1979	Price Index January 1992 (Jan. 1987 = 100)	Weight used in January 1992
Food	217.7	233	128.4	151
Catering	218.7	51	144.3	47
Alcoholic Drink	198.9	85	143.9	77
Tobacco	231.5	48	137.4	32
Housing	190.3	113	156.0	192
Fuel & Light	233.1	60	127.7	46
Household Goods (e.g. furniture)	204.4	76	123.9	70
Household Services (e.g. telephone)	219.0	26	135.3	45
Clothing & Footwear	176.1	80	115.7	63
Personal Goods & Services (e.g. toiletries)	207.4	19	138.4	38
Motoring Expenditure	212.9	116	134.0	141
Fares & Other Travel Costs	250.0	24	140.9	20
Leisure Goods (e.g. newspapers)	205.5	46	119.3	48
Leisure Services (e.g. entertainment)	170.5	23	145.5	30
ALL ITEMS	207.2	1000	135.6	1000

1 At what percentage rates did retail prices rise on average during each of the following five year periods:
   a January 1974—January 1979
   b January 1987—January 1992? (4)

2 Explain why, if the price of a commodity constantly increases at a rate of 50 per cent a year, it will take less than two years for its price to double. (4)

3 Which of the 14 broad categories of prices
   a rose most rapidly, and
   b rose least rapidly during the period January 1974—January 1979?
   Was the same true during the period January 1987—January 1992? (4)

4 Which two commodity groups increased most in relative importance between January 1979 and January 1992, and which two commodity groups decreased most in relative importance between these two dates?

5 Suggest some explanations for the trends identified in question **4**. (4)

6 Using the January 1987 base, the Index of Retail Prices was calculated to be

130.2 in January 1991. Calculate the annual inflation rate between January 1991 and January 1992. (4)

7 Using the January 1974 base, the Index of Retail Prices was calculated to be 394.5 in January 1987. By how much did UK retail prices rise on average over the 18 years between January 1974 and January 1992? How many pence was a 50p coin 'placed under the mattress' in January 1974 worth in January 1992? (5)

8 One of the main uses of the Index of Retail Prices is in calculating the annual rate of inflation, and this is often used as the basis for specific price rises, such as Public Transport Fares. Explain why the rate of inflation calculated from the UK Index of Retail Prices may be a poor indicator of average price increases in Northern Ireland. (6)

The sterling trade weighted index

The *sterling trade weighted index* is another example of a weighted average. In this case we are trying to measure changes in the value of the pound sterling against a 'basket' of other currencies. Once again we face the problem of relative importance: the value of the pound against the American dollar is of much more significance to UK firms than its value against the Swiss franc.

Consider the following hypothetical data.

Country	Weight	Exchange rate	
		1990	**1991**
USA	40	£1 = $2	£1 = $1.60
Germany	30	£1 = DM3	£1 = DM2.25
France	20	£1 = 8f	£1 = 9.6f
Switzerland	10	£1 = 2Fr	£1 = 3Fr

The weights reflect the percentage of total UK trade with the countries in question: 40 per cent of UK trade was with the USA, 30 per cent with Germany, and so on.

Between 1990 and 1991, the pound fell against the US dollar by 20 per cent ($\frac{0.40}{2.00} \times 100$) and against the German mark by 25 per cent. It rose against the French franc by 20 per cent and against the Swiss franc by 50 per cent.

Presenting this data in index number form, with 1990 as the base year, we get:

Currency	Exchange rate	
	1990	**1991**
Dollar	100	80
Mark	100	75
French franc	100	120
Swiss franc	100	150

We must now allow for the relative importance of each currency by multiplying the 1991 index by its weight:

Currency	Weight	1991 index	W × 1991 index
Dollar	40	80	3200
Mark	30	75	2250
French franc	20	120	2400
Swiss franc	10	150	1500
	Total 100		Total 9350

The final stage in obtaining the sterling trade weighted index for 1991 is to divide 9350 by 100, which gives us a figure of 93.5. The pound therefore fell against this 'basket' of currencies by 6.5 per cent.

The actual figure for the **sterling index** on 8 October 1993 was 80.9 against its base of 100 in 1980.

REAL VALUES AND MONEY VALUES

Many economic variables, for example income, output or expenditure, are measured in terms of money. Hence their value will change when there is a change in the value of money. In other words, inflation can distort the meaning of an economic variable and some technique must be found for eliminating its impact. When this adjustment has been made the variable is said to be measured in **'real'** **terms**. Hence the **real rate of interest** is the nominal rate minus the rate of inflation, and **real income** is the purchasing power of your income in comparison with what it would have bought in some previous year, known as the base year.

Consider a simple example. Suppose that in 1985 a teacher's salary had been £10 000 per year and that by 1990 it had risen to £15 000. Does it follow that the teacher is 50 per cent better off in 1990? In purely **monetary terms** the answer is obviously yes, but this does not necessarily mean that the teacher's standard of living is any higher than it was in 1985. The real income would actually have fallen if inflation between 1985 and 1990 had been greater than 50 per cent. In this case the purchasing power of £15 000 in 1990 would actually be less than that of £10 000 in 1985. In other words, to answer the original question fully, we need to be able to distinguish between real and monetary values.

Calculating real values
This is done by calculating a money variable at constant prices, that is by assuming that the prices of a base year have remained unchanged.

Consider an economy with only one product, beer.

	1990	**1991**
Output	10 gallons	12 gallons
Price per gallon	£10	£12
Money value of total output	£100	£144

We can see that the total output of this economy over the period 1990–91 has risen *in money terms* by 44 per cent from £100 to £144 but the *actual* physical production of beer has gone up by only 20 per cent, from 10 gallons to 12 gallons. The remainder of this increase has been caused by an inflationary increase in the price of a gallon of beer. Hence to get the real output in 1991 we must value the physical output of that year at the prices of 1990. This gives us 12 gallons at £10 each and total output at £120. We have therefore removed the inflationary element from the value of 1991 output simply by measuring it at constant prices.

In the above example it was quite easy to measure inflation as we had only one product to consider. In the real world a modern economy produces much more than beer, and we have to rely on the retail price index as a measure of changes in the overall price level. However, the calculation of real output is no more difficult than in the above single-product economy.

Consider the following information, taken from the 1993 Blue Book.

Year	UK GDP (£m)
1991	573 645
1992	596 165

In money terms, the UK GDP increased by £22 520 million or 3.9 per cent, which at first sight would appear to be a very satisfactory rate of economic growth for the UK economy. Alas, much of this increase is purely inflationary as we can see from the following figures for the retail price index.

Year	RPI
1991	106.5
1992	111.2

So to calculate the 1992 GDP at 1991 prices we simply multiply 1992 GDP by 1991 RPI and divide by 1992 RPI:

$$\frac{596\,165 \times 106.5}{111.2}$$
$$= 570\,967$$

We now see that real output in 1992 was £570 967 million, representing a fall of £2678 million or 0.47 per cent. This is clearly a much less impressive economic performance than the unadjusted rise of 3.9 per cent.

In the above example, the figure $\frac{106.5}{111.2}$ is known as the **GDP deflator**.

There are many situations in which it is essential to be able to calculate real as opposed to money values. Consider the following data on UK beer expenditure.

Year	Beer consumption (£m)
1988	10 039
1989	10 676
1990	11 701
1991	12 849
1992	13 267
Change 1988–92 = +32%	

On the basis of these figures a researcher investigating the UK beer market might well feel that sales were steadily increasing. However, an entirely different picture emerges when an adjustment is made for inflation by measuring sales at constant 1990 prices.

Year	Beer consumption (£m)
1988	11 779
1989	11 767
1990	11 701
1991	11 393
1992	11 046
Change 1988–92 = –6%	

Instead of a rise of 32 per cent over this five-year period we now have a 6 per cent fall. This tells us that although consumers were spending more money on beer, the number of units purchased actually fell.

INDEX-LINKING

The index-linking of pensions and other benefits is another area in which it is important to be able to assess the impact of inflation. If the purchasing power of benefits is to be protected then they must rise by at least the same percentage as the cost of living. This theme is examined in the following UCLES A level question.

THE SHOPPING BASKET OVER 50 YEARS

The following data relates to the United Kingdom between 1939 and 1989.

	1939	1949	1959	1969	1979	1989
Equivalent purchasing power of £1 then in today's money	£26.20	£13.20	£9.30	£6.60	£2.04	£1.00

(Prices below are expressed in new pence: 100 new pence = £1)

	1939	1949	1959	1969	1979	1989
Bread (large loaf 1½ lb or 800 g)	3.1	5.5	10.9	20.0	30.0	50.0
Beef (top quality) per lb	14.9	26.0	64.3	103.0	206.7	271.0
Bacon (back) per lb	15.8	31.0	58.4	76.9	115.9	162.0
Margarine (1 lb)	6.2	10.0	10.2	11.3	15.9	38.0
Milk (pint)	3.5	5.0	8.0	11.0	15.0	28.0
Butter (1 lb)	18.1	18.0	32.4	42.9	79.7	120.0
Cheese (Cheddar) 1 lb	9.9	14.0	40.7	42.4	86.9	144.0
Eggs (per dozen)	25.2	48.0	48.0	45.6	57.0	99.0
Sugar (white gran.) 1 lb	4.4	5.0	7.7	8.9	33.1	57.0
Coffee (roast) 1 lb	25.8	†	90.0	115.0	221.1	135.0
Tea 1 lb	26.7	40.0	80.4	74.4	92.0	102.0
Beer (pint)	2.5	6.0	22.3	32.8	46.9	95.0
Cigarettes (20)	5.0	17.5	47.0	62.0	67.0	150.0

† Prices not given for coffee 1947–1955 owing to shortage in supplies

Source: Sunday Telegraph, 20 August 1989

1 a How many pounds (£) were needed in 1989 to buy what the £ would buy in 1939? (1)
b In which 10 year period was the rate of inflation greatest? Explain your answer. (2)

2 Use demand and supply analysis to explain why the price of coffee behaved differently from all other commodity prices listed in the decade 1979–89. (3)

3 Which of the items shown increased *most* in price over the whole period? Use demand and supply analysis to explain why this might have happened. (4)

4 a To calculate a cost of living index it is also necessary to weight the items used in a typical shopping basket. Explain why this is necessary. (2)
b How would you expect the weight given to cigarettes to change in the future? Explain your answer. (4)
c Why would the way inflation is calculated be of significance to those who are retired and living on pensions? (4)

UCLES, June 1992

SEASONALLY ADJUSTED DATA

It is common practice to present certain data in a seasonally adjusted form. This is particularly true of unemployment, which is greatly influenced by seasonal factors. These include:

- autumn – unemployment usually rises as school-leavers can be included on the register for the first time. There is also some downturn in tourism-based jobs.
- winter – unemployment rises still further because of difficulties in working outdoors. Hence there is a downturn in agriculture and construction sectors.
- spring – unemployment starts to fall as agriculture and construction pick up once again.
- summer – unemployment falls further as tourism- and leisure-based industries employ more workers.

Users of the unemployment figures will wish to be able to identify any long-term trend. They will need to be able to distinguish between a rise which is purely seasonal and another which is an indicator of recession in the economy. Seasonally adjusted figures will enable them to do this.

Seasonally adjusting is also useful to prevent data being deliberately misinterpreted for political or other reasons.

There are various techniques by which seasonal adjustment can be achieved. The Central Statistical Office will know from past experience how much seasonal variation there should be in unemployment in any particular month. When this variation is deducted from the actual change, then we have the seasonally adjusted change in unemployment.

However, as already stated, data response papers are not statistics exams and you are not expected to be familiar with the minutiae of these techniques.

RELATIONSHIPS BETWEEN ECONOMIC VARIABLES

A skill frequently tested in data response questions is the ability to identify and explain the relationships which may exist between economic variables.

The idea of such relationships lies at the heart of much government economic policy. Politicians believe, not always correctly, that by changing one variable they can bring about a favourable movement in some other variable. For instance, it is widely held that lower interest rates will bring about higher levels of employment.

INVERSE RELATIONSHIPS

In the above example, interest rates and employment are said to be **inversely related**, as a rise in one causes a fall in the other and vice versa.

The elementary demand curve is another example of an inverse relationship between two economic variables. A rise in the price of an item from p_1 to p_2 will cause a fall in the quantity demanded from q_1 to q_2 and vice versa.

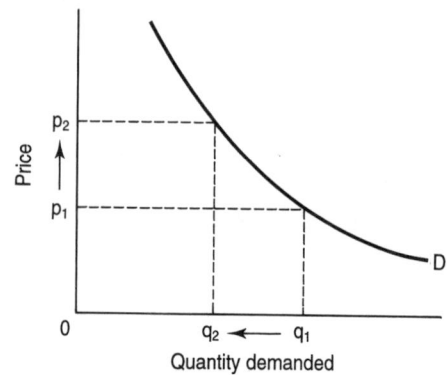

Another relationship which for many years determined government management of aggregate demand was the **Phillips curve**. This relationship, named after its author, A.W. Phillips, showed that high unemployment was associated with low inflation and low unemployment with high inflation.

For two decades after the Second World War successive governments tried, with some success, to 'slide up and down the Phillips curve'. They manipulated total spending in the economy to reach whichever combination of inflation and unemployment was deemed most suitable for economic and political reasons.

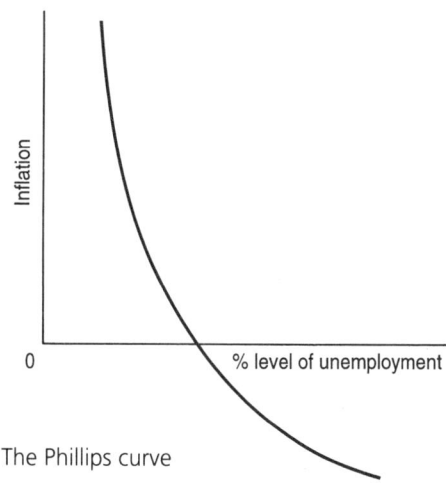

The Phillips curve

The manner in which one variable impacts upon another is known as its **transmission mechanism**. In the first example above, lower interest rates would be likely to create an increase in aggregate demand in the economy which would then lead to a rise in the number of jobs. A more technical analysis of this relationship could be developed in terms of the Keynesian marginal efficiency of capital, the level of investment expenditure, the multiplier and the deflationary gap.

DIRECT RELATIONSHIPS

When two variables rise and fall together, they are said to have a **direct**, rather than an inverse, relationship.

A simple example of this is the supply curve.

As price rises from p_1 to p_2 more of the product is offered for sale (q_2).

Another direct relationship would be that between the demand for a good and the price of a substitute product. Hence a rise in the price of Coke would be likely to cause a rise in demand for Pepsi.

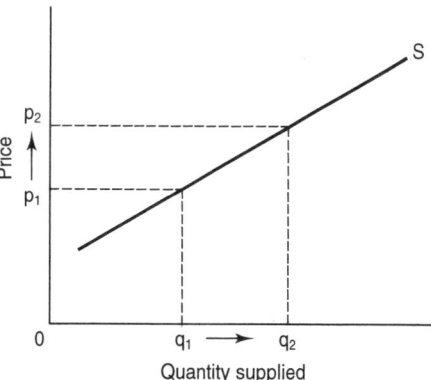

Cross-elasticity between the demand for Pepsi and the price of Coke can be defined as:

$$\frac{\% \text{ change in demand for Pepsi}}{\% \text{ change in price of Coke}}$$

For substitutes this formula will always produce a positive outcome. It will be a plus divided by a plus or a minus divided by a minus, both of which give a positive value.

Suppose the price of Coke were to rise from 25p to 30p and as a result the weekly sales of Pepsi rose from 200 000 to 250 000. The cross-elasticity of demand for Pepsi with regard to changes in the price of Coke would be calculated as follows:

$$\% \text{ change in demand for Pepsi} = +25\%$$
$$\% \text{ change in price of Coke} = +20\%$$
$$\frac{+25}{+20} = +1.25$$

A similar relationship normally exists between the value of the pound and the demand for imports. As sterling appreciates, the UK price of foreign goods falls, hence making them more attractive to UK consumers.

Consider a new BMW car costing DM45 000. If £1 exchanges for DM2, then the UK consumer will pay £22 500 for the car. However, if the pound were to rise in value to DM3 then the UK price would fall to £15 000.

The **consumption function** (right) is another example of a direct relationship between two variables, in this case consumption expenditure and disposable income.

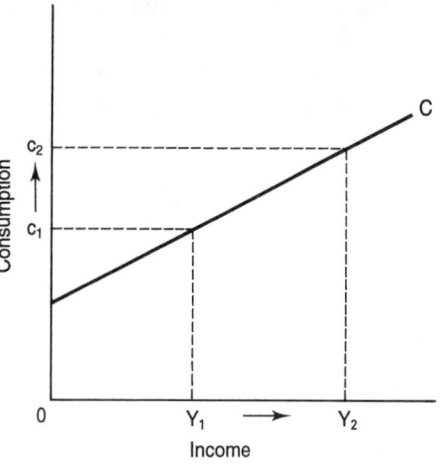

As income rises from Y_1 to Y_2 so does consumption from c_1 to c_2.

TIME LAGS

The adjustment of one variable in response to a change in some other variable will almost certainly not be immediate. There may be a substantial time lag between the two changes.

The impact of a price change on quantity demanded will, to some extent, depend upon the frequency with which the items are purchased. A change in the price of a daily newspaper will have an immediate effect on sales as consumers can adjust immediately to the new choices with which they are confronted. When the prices of the *Sun* and *The Times* newspapers were reduced, sales of the two newspapers increased significantly – showing that readers made rapid and substantial changes in purchases in response to the new lower prices.

However, changes in the prices of consumer durables, such as washing machines, only affect those who are contemplating the purchase of a washing machine at that time.

Changes in agricultural prices will influence farmers in their selection of land use. A rise in potato prices, for example, would be expected to encourage farmers to transfer resources from dairy farming. However, they would not be able to do this immediately and so, in the short run, the supply of potatoes might not be responsive to a change in price. Only in the long run, when farmers have had time to adjust, could the supply be expected to rise.

CETERIS PARIBUS

This mysterious Latin phrase is a condition upon which all the above relationships are based. It simply means 'all other things remaining unchanged'. Thus a rise in price will cause a fall in quantity demanded *so long as nothing else changes*. It would be quite possible for an increase in the price of ice-cream to be associated with a rise in demand if a heatwave were to occur at the same time as the price rise. Likewise, an increase in disposable income might occur at the same time as a fall in consumption if there were simultaneous rises in interest rates.

All of this serves to illustrate the extreme difficulty of economic forecasting. It is not easy to unravel the impact of one variable upon another and, even when it can be identified, there is no certainty that it will last for ever. The Phillips curve relationship fitted the facts between 1860 and 1956 but was not valid in the 1970s and 1980s.

Economics studies human behaviour and this is neither constant nor predictable. The *ceteris paribus* condition is not achievable in the real world and the so-called 'laws' of economics are merely tendencies. Perhaps we should be rather more understanding, then, when politicians make economic predictions which turn out to be wide of the mark!

The following extract from an AEB A level paper is a typical example of a data response question requiring you to identify relationships between variables.

Study the following data which relate to selected key economic indicators for the UK, USA, Japan and France between 1985 and 1991 and answer the questions which follow.

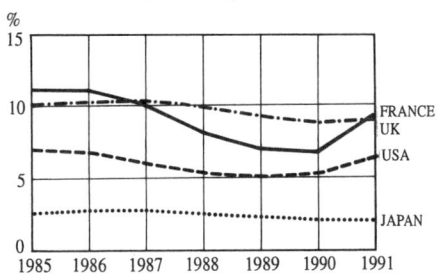

Graph 1: Index of Industrial Production   Graph 2: Unemployment Rates (% of total labour force)

Adapted from *OECD Financial Statistics*, 1992.

1 Describe and explain the possible relationships between industrial production and unemployment as shown in graphs 1 and 2.   (5)

AEB, June 1993

Exercises

1 Table 1 describes the UK's export performance between 1983 and 1992.

Table 1 UK exports, 1983–92

Year	Visible exports (£m)
1983	60 700
1984	70 265
1985	77 991
1986	72 627
1987	79 153
1988	80 346
1989	92 154
1990	101 718
1991	103 413
1992	107 047

Present the time-series data given in Table 1 in index number form, with 1985 as the base year. Call your index the UK export index.

2 Using the figures given in Table 1, change the base year for your UK export index from 1985 to 1990.

3 Table 2 shows consumer expenditure in the UK on soft drinks, measured at current market prices.

Table 2 UK consumer expenditure on soft drinks, current market prices, 1985–92

Year	Expenditure (£m)
1985	1697
1986	1962
1987	2222
1988	2499
1989	2838
1990	3198
1991	3360
1992	3503

Construct a soft drinks consumption index with 1990 as the base year.

4 Table 3 also gives information on consumer expenditure on soft drinks, but this time measured at 1990 constant prices.

Table 3 UK consumer expenditure on soft drinks, 1990 constant prices, 1985–92

Year	Expenditure (£m)
1985	2199
1986	2592
1987	2868
1988	2856
1989	3098
1990	3198
1991	3223
1992	3239

Explain the difference between the two sets of data given in Tables 2 and 3.

5 Use the information in questions **3** and **4** to calculate the RPI in each year from 1985 to 1992. Assume 1990 to be the base year.

6 Table 4 presents the output of agriculture, forestry and fishing in index number form.

Table 4   Output index for agriculture, forestry and fishing, 1981–9 (1985 = 100)

Year	Output
1981	88
1982	95
1983	90
1984	105
1985	100
1986	98
1987	99
1988	97
1989	98

a What year is the base year?
b Calculate the percentage change in output for each year from 1982 to 1989.

7 The actual output of agriculture, forestry and fishing in 1985 was £5553 million. Use this information and the index number data in Table 4 to calculate the actual output of the sector from 1981 to 1989.

8 Table 5 gives information on attendances at FA Premier League football matches.

Table 5   Attendance at FA Premier League football matches

Season	Average attendance
1988/89	20 600
1989/90	20 800
1990/91	22 681
1991/92	21 622
1992/93	21 125

a Present this information in the form of (i) a bar chart and (ii) an attendance index, with 1988/89 as the base season.
b Suggest two *economic* factors which may have contributed to the decline in attendances since the 1990/91 season.

9 Government statisticians on the island of Utopia believe that the usual seasonal trend in unemployment is as follows.

Spring	−1.8%
Summer	−2.2%
Autumn	+1.5%
Winter	+2.5%

The actual unemployment figures over a two-year period are shown in Table 6.

Table 6 Unemployment in Utopia, 1990–1

Season	Year	No unemployed
Spring	1990	10 000
Summer	1990	10 500
Autumn	1990	11 000
Winter	1990	12 000
Spring	1991	12 000
Summer	1991	11 000
Autumn	1991	11 500
Winter	1991	12 000

a Calculate the quarterly percentage change in unemployment starting with the summer of 1990.
b Calculate the seasonally adjusted change in unemployment over the same period.

10 Consider the following figures for the retail price index.

Table 7 Retail price index, 1983–8 (1985 = 100)

Year	RPI
1983	89.8
1984	94.3
1985	100
1986	103.4
1987	107.7
1988	113.0

a If a basket of goods cost £10 in 1983, how much would a similar basket cost in each of the five subsequent years?
b A different basket of goods cost £10 in 1985. How much would this basket cost in 1986, in 1987 and in 1988?

11 Unbeknown to you the tooth fairy placed a £10 note under your pillow in 1983. Using the RPI data in Table 7, calculate the real value of this stroke of good fortune if the £10 note was discovered in **a** 1984, **b** 1985, **c** 1986, **d** 1987 and **e** 1988.

12 The price elasticity of demand can be calculated by dividing the percentage change in quantity demanded by the percentage change in price.
a Ignoring the minus sign, calculate the price elasticity of demand in the following situations.
   (i) The price of a season ticket for Anfield rises from £200 to £300 and the quantity of tickets demanded falls from 10 000 to 9000.
   (ii) The price is now reduced to its original level and sales return to 10 000.
b Why are the two elasticities not identical?

13 The income elasticity of demand is calculated by dividing the percentage change in demand by the percentage change in consumers' income.
a Calculate the income elasticity of demand in the following situations.
   (i) A family's income rises from £20 000 to £25 000 per annum. As a result they eat out at local restaurants 26 times per year instead of 13 times.
   (ii) This same family reduce their consumption of Grotto cheap lager from 250 cans per year to 150 cans per year.
b Explain the meaning of the minus sign in your answer to **a** (ii).

14 Table 8 shows the pattern of attendances at five major sporting events since 1981.

Table 8 Attendances at major sporting events (thousands), 1981–93

Event	Attendances (000s)			
	1981	**1986**	**1991**	**1993**
Wimbledon	358	400	354	393
The Grand National	56	53	56	50
The Derby	50	47	26	27
Varsity rugby match	28	38	57	66
Open golf championship	112	134	192	140

a Describe the trend in attendance at each of the five events over the 12-year period.
b Identify the event with the highest percentage increase and that with the highest percentage decrease.

15 The following data describes the trend in trade union membership in the UK since 1981.

Table 9 Trade union membership in the UK, 1981–91

Year	Total membership (millions)	Membership as % of civilian workforce in employment
1981	12.1	50.4
1982	11.6	49.2
1983	11.2	48.2
1984	11.0	45.4
1985	10.8	44.5
1986	10.5	43.0
1987	10.5	41.4
1988	10.4	39.8
1989	10.2	38.1
1990	9.9	37.7
1991	9.6	37.7

a Construct an index of trade union membership with 1981 as the base year. What is the percentage fall in trade union membership over this period?
b Calculate the size of the civilian workforce in employment for each of the years 1981–91.

Answers to these exercises are printed on pages 143–8.

Chapter 2

Common themes in data response questions

Although in theory the data could refer to any topic, in practice examiners tend to concentrate on topical issues. The more media space devoted to a theme the more likely it is to have caught the attention of the examiner. However, remember that questions are usually set at least a year in advance and so 'topical' may mean what was topical last year!

Inflation

Inflation is usually defined as **a sustained rise in the general level of prices**. Control of inflation is a major objective of government economic policy. It is scarcely possible to read any quality newspaper without finding some reference to this topic.

HERE SADIE, I WISH THEY'D GET THIS INFLATION SORTED OUT. MY ARMS ARE SORE CARRYING THIS BARROW TO THE SUPERMARKET.

It is important that you are familiar with the different ways in which inflation is measured. This is by no means straightforward. When we talk about 'the general level of prices', which prices are we referring to? Do we mean retail prices or wholesale prices? Should we include the price of every product or simply those products which most people buy on a regular basis? How do we deal with new products or significant improvements in the quality of existing ones? All of this makes the measurement of inflation an extremely complex area and explains why a number of different indices are used for this purpose. The most commonly used is the **retail price index** (see page 9).

COMPILING THE RETAIL PRICE INDEX

The RPI aims to measure changes in 'the cost of living'. This immediately poses the problem of what exactly we mean by the phrase 'cost of living'. If there is a large rise in the price of beer, then heavy drinkers will face a substantial rise in their cost of living whilst teetotallers will not suffer at all! Thus each of us will have a slightly different 'cost of living', depending upon our tastes, preferences and circumstances.

A typical pattern of expenditure for the average household is constructed by the Family Expenditure Survey. Certain groups such as the very rich, the very poor and pensioners are excluded from the survey because their spending pattern would be unrepresentative of a typical household. A separate price index is calculated for pensioners.

The total number of respondents for the Family Expenditure Survey in the three years 1989–91 is given below.

	1989	1990	1991
Total respondent households	7410	7046	7056
Average number of persons per household	2.51	2.48	2.42

From this survey data we can calculate the percentage of total spending allocated to each of the 14 product groups, and this gives us the weights.

Prices are monitored throughout the UK and inflation figures are published each month; inflation here being expressed as the percentage change in the RPI.

USES OF THE RPI: INDEX-LINKING AND PRICE FORMULAS

The change in the cost of living is regarded by the government as the annual percentage change in the RPI. This refers to the percentage change in the RPI from the same month in the previous year.

	1992	1993
September	139.4	141.9
October	139.9	141.8

Hence the annual inflation figure, measured in September 1993, is

$$\frac{141.9 - 139.4}{139.4} \times 100 = 1.79\%$$

This measurement of the change in the cost of living is used to adjust a large number of variables in order to maintain their real value. This is known as **index-linking**.

- **Social welfare benefits** Many social security benefits are increased each year in line with inflation. The increases take place in April and are based on the annual rise in the RPI for the year ending in the previous September. Hence recipients of benefits such as child benefit lose out in periods of rising inflation but gain when inflation is falling.
- **Index-linked gilts** Holders of index-linked gilts are always guaranteed a positive *real* interest rate. The return is usually set at inflation plus 2 per cent. These investors do very well when inflation is high but much less well when inflation is low. In September 1993, for example, the Treasury issued a 'tranche' (or batch) of 11-year gilts at 6.75 per cent. At the same time the rate of inflation was only 1.8 per cent, giving holders of index-linked gilts a return of 3.8 per cent. It would require inflation to rise to 4.75 per cent before the holders of the index-linked gilts would fare better than the holders of the 11-year gilts.
- **Index-linked pensions** Retired government employees, for example teachers and civil servants, receive a pension which is upgraded each year in line with inflation.
- **Pricing policies of public utilities** The main public utilities, such as gas, electricity and water distribution, are natural monopolies. In the absence of effective competition the interests of customers are protected by a regulator who has the power to set limits on the level of price increases in the industry. In most cases a price formula is set and this is usually based on the RPI. British Gas, for instance, is not permitted to raise its prices by more than the rise in the RPI minus 5 per cent.
- **Capital gains tax liability** Profits earned on the sale of assets such as shares, antiques and second homes are taxed as capital gains. However, tax is levied only on *real* gains, that is over and above the rate of inflation. In order to calculate these real gains every year the Inland Revenue produces indexation tables based on the RPI.

It is clear that a number of practical day-to-day activities require an accurate measure of changes in the cost of living.

28

ALTERNATIVE MEASURES OF INFLATION

As well as the RPI, other indices used to measure inflation are the following.

THE PRODUCER PRICE INDEX (PPI)

This measures changes in the prices paid by firms when purchasing commodities from other firms. The PPI can be used to give advance warning of impending changes in retail prices.

PENSIONER PRICE INDEX

This is prepared for one- and two-person households. Since pensioners spend proportionately more on items such as heating and less on those such as motoring, the weights attached to each category of expenditure are significantly different from those used in the RPI.

THE TAX AND PRICES INDEX (TPI)

This measure of inflation was much quoted by government spokespersons in the early 1980s when most direct tax rates were falling and indirect taxes such as VAT were being increased. So taxpayers found that they had a higher disposable income through paying less income tax, but their cost of living had gone up because of rises in VAT.

It was felt that the RPI gave a misleading picture of the change in circumstances of the average family, since it included changes in retail prices without making allowance for the beneficial impact of lower rates of income tax. Hence the TPI was defined as the change in gross income that the average income earner would require to maintain his or her standard of living.

Suppose in the base year Mr Average has a gross income of £10 000, from which the state deducts £2000 (20 per cent) in tax and National Insurance, leaving him with disposable income of £8000. The following year deductions are reduced to 15 per cent and retail prices rise by 10 per cent. How much of a rise in gross pay does Mr Average need in order to keep real income unchanged?

Clearly he requires a 10 per cent rise in his disposable income to £8800 in order to keep pace with inflation. But this does not mean that he should get a 10 per cent rise in gross income, for the tax reductions have already increased his disposable income to £8500. To maintain his real income he needs a gross income of £10 353, because £8800 is 85 per cent of gross income (that is gross income minus tax at 15 per cent). Hence gross income required is

$$\frac{£8800}{85} \times 100 = £10\,353$$

Thus a rise of £353 or 3.53 per cent would leave his standard of living unchanged.

$$\text{gross income} = £10\,353$$
$$\text{tax (15\%)} = £1553$$
$$\text{disposable pay} = £8800$$
$$\text{real disposable income in year 2} = £8800 \times \frac{\text{RPI (year 1)}}{\text{RPI (year 2)}}$$
$$= £8800 \times \frac{100}{110}$$
$$= £8000$$

So disposable income in year 2 is exactly the same in real terms as it was in year 1. In other words, Mr Average's standard of living has been maintained by a rise in income of only 3.53 per cent, in spite of the fact that the RPI has risen by 10 per cent.

UNDERLYING INFLATION OR RPI(X)

It has become fashionable for government spokespersons to distinguish between **headline inflation** and **underlying inflation**. This is particularly common when so-called underlying inflation is significantly lower than the headline figure.

Headline inflation is simply the normally accepted measure of inflation, that is the annual percentage rise in the RPI. Underlying inflation is this figure with changes in housing costs removed. It is often referred to as **RPI(X)**.

The rationale for this distinction is that any rise in inflation will usually trigger a rise in interest rates, which automatically causes a rise in the cost of repaying a mortgage. With the cost of housing included in the RPI, there is a corresponding rise in inflation. Hence a government policy to defeat inflation (by raising interest rates) automatically has the reverse effect. This is regarded as a distortion, and the government prefers forecasters and commentators to concentrate on the underlying rate of inflation.

When interest rates and housing costs are lower, less attention is paid to underlying inflation, although it remains a target of monetary policy.

RPI(Y)

The development of a measure known as **RPI(Y)** is a further extension of this attempt to distinguish between price rises that are the result of government policy and those that occur because of excess spending in the economy. This measure excludes not only mortgage interest repayments but also the impact of changes in indirect taxation such as the imposition of 8 per cent VAT on domestic fuel.

POST-WAR TRENDS IN INFLATION

In 1993, UK inflation was at historically low levels. In September the annual rate was 1.8 per cent and in October it fell even further to 1.4 per cent. Although now rising, it is still at comparatively low levels. This represents a remarkable turnaround in the British economy.

Consider the following figures for inflation in the UK during the 1970s.

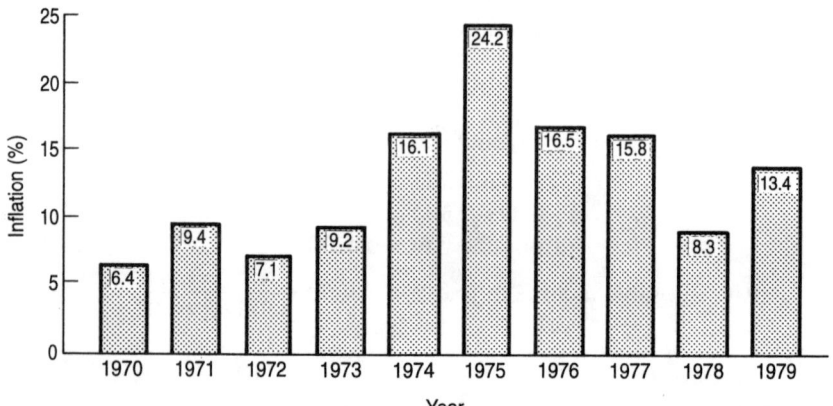

The election of the Conservative government under Margaret Thatcher in 1979 brought a monetarist zeal to the defeat of inflation which was soon reflected in the figures:

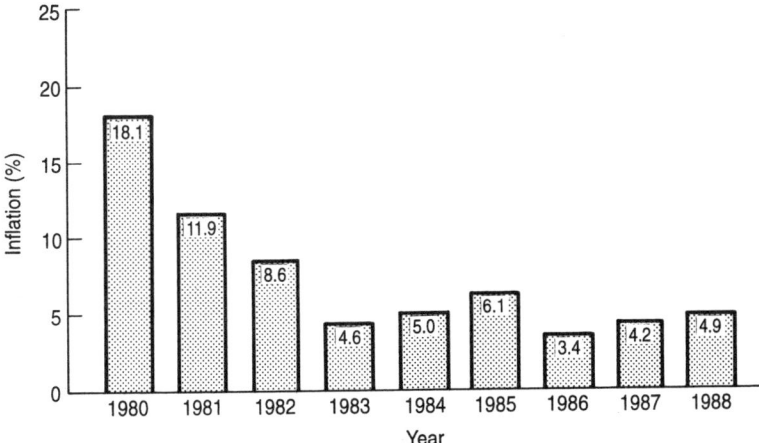

By 1988 both Mrs Thatcher and the chancellor, Mr Lawson, must have been feeling rather smug: inflation was low and unemployment had at last started to fall. Add to this a resounding victory in the 1987 general election and both could have been forgiven for feeling that their hold on power was indeed firm.

However, as history demonstrates, rulers are most vulnerable when they feel most secure. That slight rise in inflation which first appeared in 1987 continued into 1988 and then accelerated. In 1989 it reached 7.7 per cent and rose still further in 1990 to 9.5 per cent. Corrective measures in the form of a severe tightening of monetary policy had to be taken, precipitating the country into deep recession. The counter-inflationary policies achieved their desired objective, but at terrible cost in terms of higher unemployment.

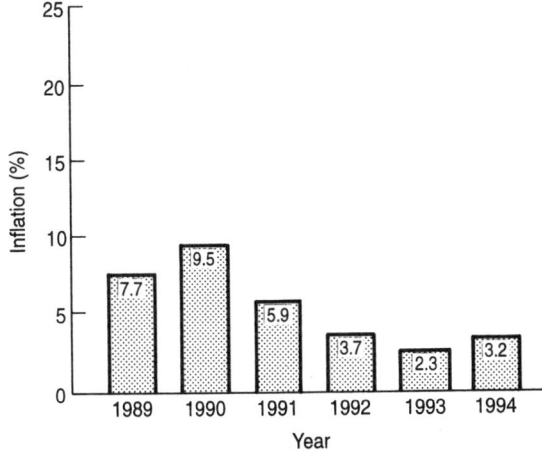

January 1995 saw the RPI 3.3 per cent higher than in January 1994. It remains to be seen whether this slight rise is a 'one-off' or part of a longer term trend towards higher inflation.

The following question from a Scottish Higher Economics paper is a typical one on inflation.

Study the passage given below, then answer the questions.

UK inflation rates 1980–1989 (based on price levels at the end of the year)

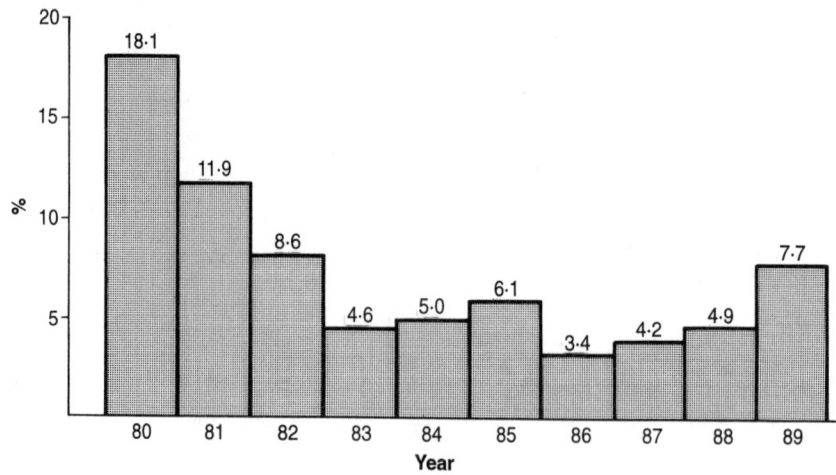

In the 1980s, a major aim of UK government policy was to achieve and maintain a low rate of inflation.

As the chart above shows, at the end of 1989 the Retail Price Index (RPI) was 7.7% higher than a year earlier. What the chart does not show is that in June 1989 the RPI had been 8.3% higher than in June 1988. By December 1989, therefore, the inflation rate was in fact decreasing.

During late 1989 inflationary pressures were starting to build up. A recent upturn in economic activity had led to shortages in markets for skilled labour, and in December 1989 the government warned trade unions against lodging wage claims that were not linked to increased labour productivity. Burdened with high interest rates, leading industrialists were urging the government to allow the exchange rate to fall. However, the government indicated that UK interest rates were likely to remain high, given the sustained growth in consumer borrowing and the continuing UK balance of trade deficit.

By the end of 1989, some political and economic commentators were questioning whether the sacrifices that had been made to bring inflation down had been worthwhile.

1 On the evidence of the chart, was the UK government able to achieve and maintain a low UK rate of inflation in the 1980s? Explain your answer. (3)

2 At the end of 1984, an enthusiastic government supporter spoke about the government's success in bringing down prices in the years 1981–4. How accurate was his observation? Explain your answer. (3)

3 Explain what is meant by a 'Retail Price Index'. (3)

4 If the RPI was at 103.4 on 31 December 1986, what had been its level on 31 December 1985? (1)

5 The passage indicates that at a time when inflation, as measured by changes in the RPI, was starting to fall, inflationary pressures were starting to build up. Explain why it is possible for inflation to fall at a time of rising inflationary pressures. (3)

6 Explain why an upturn in economic activity may lead to large wage claims by groups of skilled workers. (3)

7 Why are wage claims that are linked to improved labour productivity considered to be less inflationary than those that are not linked to improved labour productivity? (4)

8 Why might a government which was determined to bring down the rate of inflation be reluctant to allow the exchange rate to fall? (3)

9 How might a falling exchange rate make life a bit easier for some industrialists? (2)

10 What sacrifices, if any, do you consider were made in the 1980s in order to bring down the UK rate of inflation? (5)

Unemployment

As with inflation, unemployment also presents great difficulties of definition and measurement. At the time of writing, to be classified as unemployed, a person must satisfy three criteria:

- they must not be in employment
- they must be actively seeking a job and be available to take such employment if it becomes available
- they must be claiming benefit.

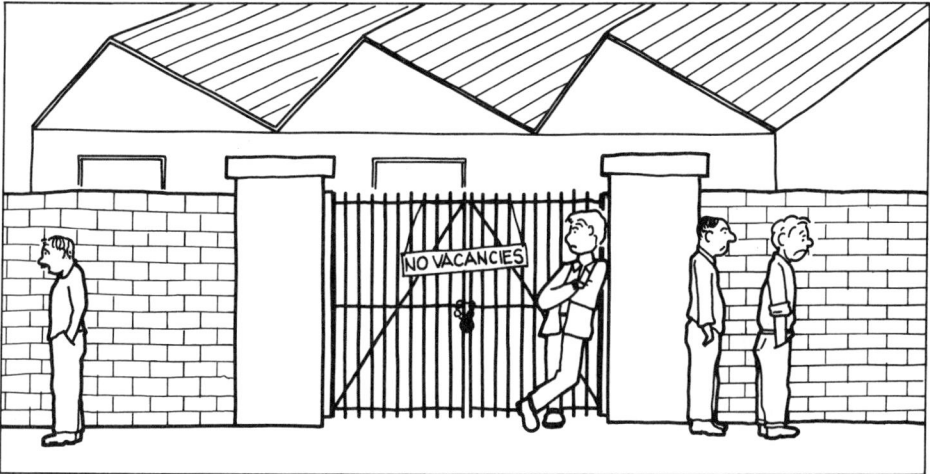

Unemployment figures are collected by the Department of Employment on the second Thursday of each month. The figures for all those registered as unemployed and claiming benefit are gathered from each area office and totalled to get the national figure.

But is this accurate? Many would think not. Mr Peter Stibbard, Director of Statistics at the Department of Employment, points out (*The Financial Times*, 29 October 1993) that there are 1 million people excluded from the register who would be included in the broader International Labour Organisation definition of unemployment. These are:

- young persons, not on Youth Training Schemes, who are not eligible for benefit
- married women who are not eligible for benefit because of their partner's earnings
- those on sickness and invalidity benefit who are regarded as not being available for work.

Left-wing critics argue that the official definition of unemployment has been changed several times since 1979 and that current figures would be 1 million higher if they were calculated in the same way as they were before 1982.

Criticism is not confined to the political left. Many free market economists also regard the data as highly suspect, but for different reasons. They argue that many people 'signing on' are not actually available for work; they are active in the black economy and are much better off than they would be in full-time employment. The ILO definition excludes such claimants but they are included in the UK government figures.

PRESENTING THE FIGURES

Unemployment figures are usually presented as a *percentage of the working population*. In September 1994 UK average unemployment was 9.1 per cent.

The term 'working population' means all those who are in full-time employment plus all those who are available for such employment. It excludes those who are either too old or too young to work plus those in full-time education.

Hence the percentage unemployed is:

$$\frac{\text{all registered claimants}}{\text{the working population}} \times \frac{100}{1}$$

Remember that the unemployed are included in the working population.

POST-WAR TRENDS IN UNEMPLOYMENT

Any writer on economics in the 1950s and 1960s would scarcely have believed that unemployment levels of over 10 per cent would have been commonplace in the UK in the 1980s and 1990s. The Beveridge Report of 1944 urged governments to aim at a level of unemployment of no more than 3 per cent, and between 1953 and 1969 unemployment never exceeded 2.6 per cent.

In the 1970s things began to go badly wrong and the UK saw both unemployment and inflation rising simultaneously.

Period	Average unemployment (%)
1970–4	2.9
1975–9	5.1

The Conservative government elected in 1979 brought the defeat of inflation, not unemployment, to the top of the political agenda. It became the accepted view that unemployment could not be tackled in isolation and that low inflation was an essential precondition for low unemployment. Thatcherism meant farewell to the Phillips curve and the existence of some kind of simple 'trade-off' between inflation and unemployment, allowing chancellors to choose between various levels of these two economic evils.

Throughout the early 1980s, as inflation fell, unemployment continued to rise.

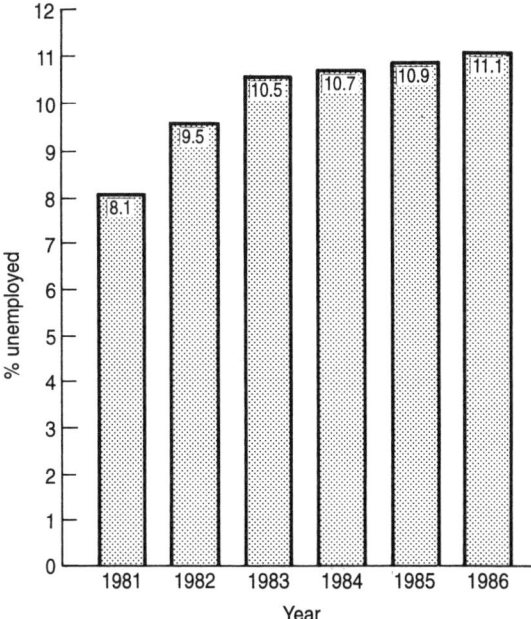

1987 saw the beginning of what subsequently became known as the 'Lawson boom'. Unemployment fell, but inflation began to rise and brakes, in the form of higher interest rates, had to be applied to the economy.

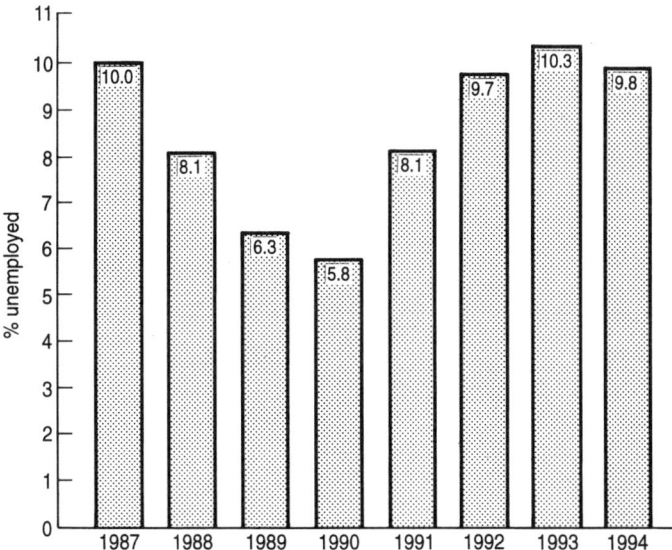

The boom was followed by a recession that proved longer and deeper than Treasury forecasters had anticipated, with unemployment rising to over 10 per cent.

However, recovery did eventually come and unemployment fell much earlier in the economic cycle than it did in the recession of the early 1980s. By June 1994 it had reached 9.4 per cent.

If unemployment has become much less of a lagging economic indicator, then this can be attributed to the greater flexibility in the labour market brought about by various supply-side reforms such as the abolition of wages councils.

REGIONAL DISTRIBUTION OF UNEMPLOYMENT

The recession of the early 1990s brought about a remarkable change in the way in which unemployment was spread throughout the UK.

Many students have images of a poor North, with declining smoke-stack industries and high unemployment. There is an equally widespread belief that the South is a region of wealth and job opportunities. Unemployment figures for the 1980s would have supported these views. Consider the following figures for 1989.

Region	% unemployed (1989)
England	
North	9.9
Yorkshire & Humberside	7.4
East Midlands	5.4
East Anglia	3.6
South-East	3.9
Greater London	5.1
Rest of South-East	2.9
South-West	4.5
West Midlands	6.6
North-West	8.5
All of England	5.6
Wales	7.3
Scotland	9.3
Northern Ireland	14.6
All of UK	6.3

These figures confirm such a traditional picture, with England in general and the South of England in particular faring much better than Scotland, Wales and Northern Ireland. However, the impact of the recession of the early 1990s was most severe in the most prosperous areas. Consider the following unemployment figures for January 1993.

Region	% unemployed (Jan. 1993)
England	
North	12.1
Yorkshire & Humberside	10.6
East Midlands	9.7
East Anglia	8.6
South-East	10.5
Greater London	11.7
Rest of South-East	9.5
South-West	10.0
West Midlands	11.5
North-West	10.9
All of England	10.6
Wales	10.3
Scotland	9.9
Northern Ireland	14.7
All of UK	10.6

Readers can immediately see that unemployment in January 1993 in both Scotland and Wales was lower than in England. Indeed Greater London had one of the highest unemployment rates in the UK, being exceeded only by the North of England and by Northern Ireland. In 1993, the once prosperous South-East had a higher rate of unemployment than Scotland: a statistic which would no doubt have brought a wry smile to the face of Rab C. Nesbitt.

The figures for 1995, however, might have caused Rab to smile rather less heartily, for although Scotland continued to have unemployment at a rate below the UK average, the gap was much narrower – indicating, perhaps, a re-emergence of the traditional North/South divide.

Region	% unemployed (Jan. 1995)
England	
North	10.8
Yorkshire & Humberside	8.9
East Midlands	8.0
East Anglia	6.5
South-East	8.2
Greater London	10.0
South-West	7.5
West Midlands	8.5
North-West	8.7
Wales	8.5
Scotland	8.4
Northern Ireland	12.2
All of UK	8.5

The following question from a NICCEA A level paper deals with the regional distribution of unemployment.

This question is based on an article by Rachel Johnson which appeared in *The Financial Times* on Friday 18 January 1991. It was written on the day after the UK unemployment statistics for December 1990 were released. Study the passage carefully and then answer the questions which follow.

The pain of unemployment spreads

Yesterday's 80,400 monthly rise in unemployment, the biggest for a decade, has confirmed fears that the numbers out of work might top 2.5m this year. The unexpectedly big December increase has provoked accusations that the government is sacrificing the 'real' economy – businesses and people – in order to achieve slower inflation. Unadjusted for seasonal variations, the numbers out of work jumped by 122,300 – the fifth-biggest monthly increase in history.

The government's high interest rate policy savaged company profits right from the very start of the recession last year. Companies' gross trading profits dropped 7.8 per cent in the third quarter. To protect remaining profits, companies are now seeking to reduce manpower. Mr Bill Martin, economist at UBS Phillips and Drew, says: 'By cutting labour, companies will effectively transfer the burden of adjustment from themselves on to households, thus completing the circle of deflation.'

Yesterday's figures showed that unemployment is spreading to all UK regions and affecting men and women alike. It is cutting into jobs in the service sector in Greater London and the South-East even more cruelly than in the manufacturing areas of the North of England and the Midlands.

It appears that redundancies are only just beginning, because the labour market is a lagging indicator of economic activity. All the evidence that the UK is in a deepening recession will mean even bigger rises in unemployment figures to come. Next month's figures are expected to disclose the largest-ever rise in unadjusted unemployment on record – about 150,000.

There are however some encouraging signs. Wage inflation is slowly easing. With demand flat, employers have been unable to pass on higher costs to the consumer and have been forced to curb wage packets instead. Some groups of workers have been prepared to accept awards based on a prospective inflation rate rather than the present 9.7 per cent. As lower pay squeezes down inflation – the government's chief economic objective – unemployment will start to fall again.

Figure 1 Regional unemployment rates

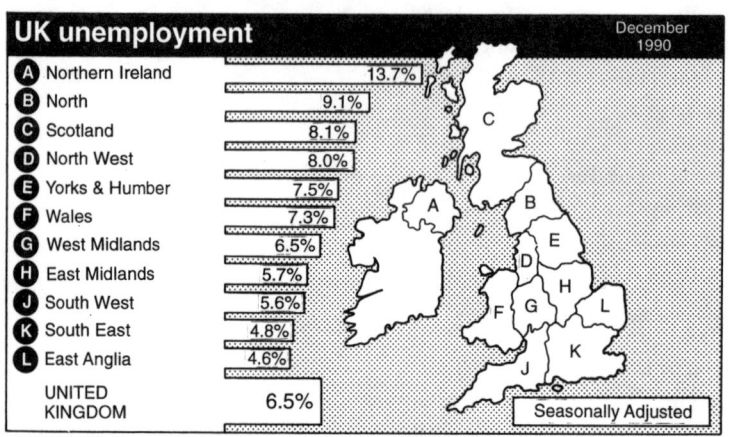

UK unemployment — December 1990

	Region	Rate
A	Northern Ireland	13.7%
B	North	9.1%
C	Scotland	8.1%
D	North West	8.0%
E	Yorks & Humber	7.5%
F	Wales	7.3%
G	West Midlands	6.5%
H	East Midlands	5.7%
J	South West	5.6%
K	South East	4.8%
L	East Anglia	4.6%
	UNITED KINGDOM	6.5%

Seasonally Adjusted

From *The Financial Times*

1 The first paragraph refers to the 'real' economy. Explain the meaning of this term, and why inflation is not regarded as a 'real' economic variable. (6)

2 Carefully explain why the seasonally adjusted increase in unemployment for December 1990 (80 400) was less than the unadjusted increase (122 300). (4)

3 Why do economists tend to be more interested in seasonally adjusted unemployment rates (as shown for example in the map in Figure 1) than in the actual rates? (5)

4 The second paragraph suggests that high interest rates have cut company profits. Why should this be so? (4)

5 Explain the meaning of the statement made by Mr Bill Martin in the second paragraph. (4)

6 Why does the third paragraph lead one to suspect that there may be less regional variation in unemployment rates in the future? (4)

7 The fourth paragraph claims that 'the labour market is a lagging indicator of economic activity'. Explain the meaning of this claim. (4)

8 The final paragraph states that 'some groups of workers have been prepared to accept awards based on a prospective inflation rate'. What does this statement mean? (4)

9 The passage ends by suggesting that a reduction in the rate of inflation will lead to a fall in unemployment rates. Outline the reasoning behind this suggestion. (5)

The balance of payments

The balance of payments is defined in the Pink Book as 'a record of transactions between residents of the UK and residents overseas'. Such transactions may be classified as:

• visible trade
• invisible trade
• transactions in external assets and liabilities.

VISIBLE TRADE

This term refers simply to trade in goods, that is items that can be seen and touched and have a physical, tangible existence. It includes items as diverse as whisky, oil, cars, agricultural produce and so on.

The **visible balance**, otherwise known as the **balance of trade**, is simply the difference between visible exports and visible imports. It can be positive or negative. A deficit occurs when the total cost of imports exceeds the total revenue from exports; a surplus is the other way round.

visible exports – visible imports = visible balance (balance of trade)

TYPES OF VISIBLE TRADE

The Pink Book classifies trade under seven headings:

1 Food, beverages and tobacco
2 Basic materials
3 Oil
4 Other minerals, fuels and lubricants
5 Semi-manufactured goods
6 Finished manufactured goods
7 Commodities which cannot be classified.

In 1979, the UK had an overall trade deficit of £3342 million and surpluses in categories 5, 6 and 7. In 1992, the overall deficit had grown to £13 046 million and there was a surplus only in oil and in commodities which cannot be classified.

GEOGRAPHICAL ANALYSIS OF TRADE

The European Union is the UK's largest trading partner. In 1992, total UK exports were £107 047 million and of this £60 365 million went to other EU countries.

Outside the EU most exports went to North America, with a value of £13 975 million.

The distribution of imports was broadly similar.

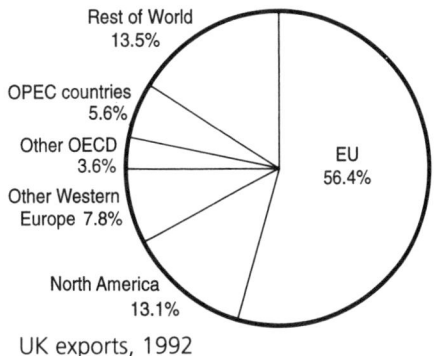

Rest of World 13.5%
OPEC countries 5.6%
Other OECD 3.6%
Other Western Europe 7.8%
North America 13.1%
EU 56.4%

UK exports, 1992

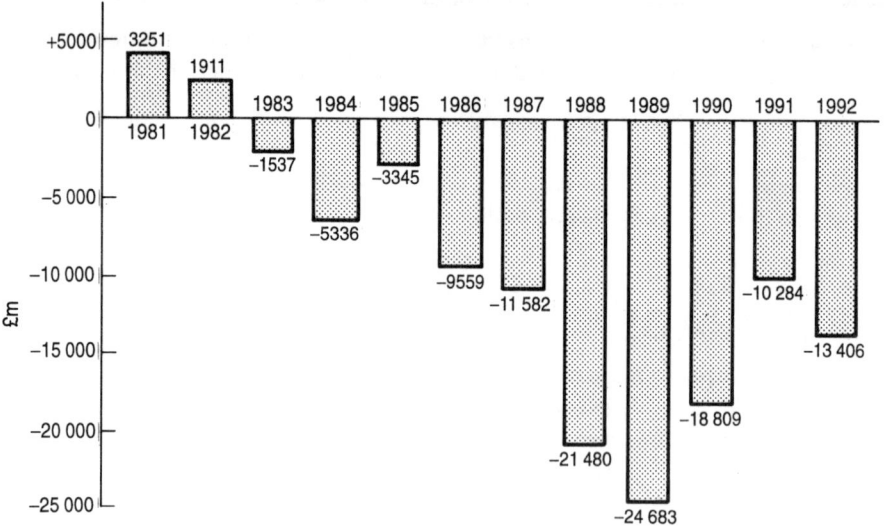

UK balance of trade, 1981–92 (£m)

This is a fairly dismal picture! The only period of surplus was during the recession of the early 1980s, and this was brought to an abrupt end by the Lawson boom. Even the 1990s recession has failed to restore a surplus, with the deficit stubbornly persisting.

INVISIBLE TRADE

There are three categories of invisible trade:

- services
- interest, profits and dividends
- transfers.

SERVICES

Credits or exports are earned when a UK firm sells a service of some sort to foreign residents. Services include the following.

- **Sea transport** This refers to the carriage of passengers and goods, and related activities such as the chartering of ships, etc. An export in this category would be a foreign manufacturer chartering a UK ship to transport its goods; an example of an import would be a UK citizen booking a cruise with a foreign shipping line. This category of transaction is usually a debit item for the UK.

Year	1988	1989	1990	1991	1992
Balance (£m)	-241	-257	-312	-283	-397

- **Civil aviation** This covers exactly the same range of activities but for planes rather than ships. It was a net earner for the UK until 1985 when there was a surplus of £201 million. Since 1986 it has been a substantial debit item.

Year	1988	1989	1990	1991	1992
Balance (£m)	-911	-528	-295	-384	-547

- **Financial and other services** This relates to banking, insurance, stockbroking, fund management, advertising, etc. It is normally a very substantial export earner for Britain with the largest single item being insurance broking.

Year	1988	1989	1990	1991	1992
Balance (£m)	8942	8812	8905	9386	10572

- **Travel** This refers to goods and services provided to UK residents while they are abroad and to foreign residents while they are in the UK. Hence the spending of an American tourist in London is an export, whilst that of Manchester United fans in Turkey is an import. Given the nature of the British climate it is hardly surprising that British citizens spend considerably more on travel abroad than the UK receives from foreign visitors.

Year	1988	1989	1990	1991	1992
Balance (£m)	-2032	-2412	-2131	-2666	-3404

- **General government** This refers to expenditure abroad by the UK government and to expenditure in the UK by foreign governments. The most common items are the upkeep of embassies and the stationing of troops. In 1992 the cost of stationing British troops in other countries came to £2114 million and of this £1207 million related to troops in Germany. Overall this item is generally a substantial debit item.

Year	1988	1989	1990	1991	1992
Balance (£m)	-1801	-2254	-2359	-2396	-2155

INTEREST, PROFITS AND DIVIDENDS

This category of invisible trade refers to the return on UK assets in other countries minus the payments to foreign holders of UK-based assets.

If a UK citizen held American government securities, then the interest received would be an invisible credit for the UK. Conversely, if an American resident held shares in Marks & Spencer then their dividend payment would be an invisible debit for the UK.

It is important to note that this category does not include the actual purchase of the asset from which the return is derived - in other words, it is not the *purchase* of the American government securities or the Marks & Spencer shares but the *returns* from them.

You should also note that this item represents the same flow of funds as that denoted by 'net property income from abroad' in the Blue Book. It is almost always a substantial credit item for the UK.

Year	1988	1989	1990	1991	1992
Balance (£m)	4424	3388	1630	320	5777

The very low figure for 1991 was the result of the high interest rates which then existed in the UK. This attracted large sums from overseas depositors into British banks and the payment of large amounts of interest to other countries.

TRANSFERS

Transfers represent payments that are neither purchases nor investments, nor even the return on investments. They are a straightforward transfer of wealth from one country to another or to some international body such as NATO, the United Nations or the European Union.

Most such transactions are made by the government. In 1992, net transfers by government were £5060 million, of which £1987 million went to EU institutions. By contrast, in 1992 net transfers by the private sector came to only £275 million.

The overall balance on transfers is generally a debit item for the UK.

Year	1988	1989	1990	1991	1992
Balance (£m)	-3518	-4578	-4897	-1345	-5060

THE BALANCE OF INVISIBLES

This is the total of the net balances in the three categories of invisible trade. The figures for 1991 are given below.

	£m
Services balance	3657
Interest, profits and dividends balance	320
Transfers balance	-1345
Invisibles balance	2632

The UK balance of invisibles is almost always in surplus and has to some extent helped to counterbalance the generally negative visible balance.

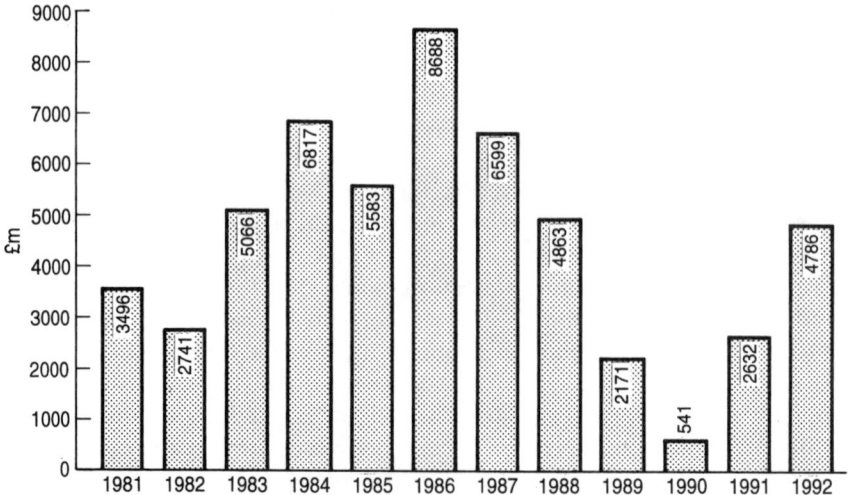

UK balance of invisibles, 1981–92 (£m)

THE CURRENT ACCOUNT BALANCE

This is the total of the visible balance and the invisible balance. Consider the following figures for 1992.

	£m
Visible balance	-13 406
Invisibles balance	4 786
Current balance	-8 620

In 1992 there was a deficit on the current account. This is sometimes referred to as a **balance of payments deficit**. If such a deficit appeared to be long lasting, then this would require some form of corrective action by government. Historical evidence would suggest that the quickest way to eliminate a balance of payments deficit is to create a recession, which is rather like amputating your arm to cure a boil on your finger! The cure is clearly worse than the ailment.

Consider the following figures for the UK balance of payments.

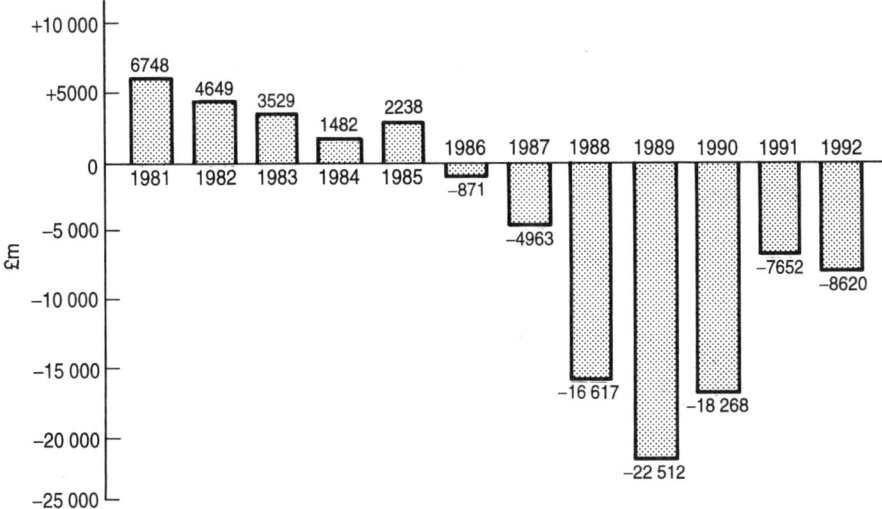

UK balance of payments, 1981–92

The figures show a relatively healthy trading performance until 1986. This was the result of the recession of the early 1980s. Recessions are good for the balance of payments because they reduce demand for imports and exert downward pressure on wage demands, hence making exports more competitive. The impact of the Lawson boom can be seen in the figures from 1987 onwards, with the deficit reaching its nadir in 1989. Thereafter the 1990s recession began to take effect and the deficit has been much reduced. However, the fact that the deficit has not been totally eliminated by the deepest recession since the 1930s must be a matter of some concern to the government.

TRANSACTIONS IN EXTERNAL ASSETS AND LIABILITIES

External assets are items of value, situated abroad, but owned by UK residents. When UK citizens and firms buy such assets in other countries this represents an outflow of funds from the UK. Hence these transactions have a minus sign in the balance of payments accounts. This does not, however, imply that such investment is 'bad' for the UK because in future years it should generate an income which would appear in the current account under 'interest, dividends and profits'.

External liabilities are the exact reverse. They represent assets, based in the UK, but owned by persons and firms in other countries. Clearly the purchase of such assets is an inflow of funds into the UK and it has a plus sign in the accounts.

Transactions in external assets and liabilities are sometimes called **capital flows**.

TYPES OF FOREIGN INVESTMENT

- **Direct investment** This includes UK firms setting up or expanding overseas subsidiaries, and foreign firms doing the same in the UK. Appropriate examples would be Japanese car manufacturers setting up plants in the UK or a British firm establishing a branch in the USA.
- **Portfolio investment** This refers to investment in government, local government and company securities.
- **Lending to overseas residents by UK banks**
- **Deposits and lending overseas by UK residents, other than banks and government** This would include deposits placed in Swiss banks by UK citizens, seeking to avoid the attention of the Inland Revenue! A more legitimate example would be a UK citizen buying a bond issued by an American firm.
- **Changes in official reserves** The official reserves consist primarily of gold and convertible foreign currencies. An increase in these is treated as a debit (or minus) in the accounts just as an increase in any other foreign-based asset is also treated as an outflow. Likewise a fall in the official reserves is treated as an inflow or credit.

The Pink Book for 1993 records the following information for 1992.

Transactions in UK assets and liabilities

	£m
UK external assets	-84 976
UK external liabilities	93 295
	8 319

THE BALANCING ITEM

There is one final item needed to complete the balance of payments, but since it is not a financial transaction it is referred to separately. This is the **balancing item**, a device by which the Central Statistical Office ensures that the accounts actually balance. It is described in the Pink Book as 'the item included to bring the sum of all the balances to zero'. This makes it sound like a method of 'cooking the books', but in theory the balance of payments should always balance and all the transactions should sum to zero.

BALANCING ACCOUNTS

The national accounts are similar to an individual's accounts. Consider the accounts of 'Andy' for the month of December 1993.

Salary	£1000
Expenditure	-£1200
Deficit	-£200

Now, if Andy was able to spend £200 more than he earned, then the money must have come from somewhere. He could have borrowed it or perhaps drawn on his past savings. If he borrowed, and if this loan were included in his accounts, then the total would come to zero.

Deficit	-£200
Loan	+£200
Total	0

Andy's deficit is similar to a current account deficit in the balance of payments; the loan in the balance of payments would be classified as an 'increase in an external liability'. Hence, in theory, any deficit or surplus on the current account would be matched by a similar transaction in the capital account.

WHY DO WE NEED A BALANCING ITEM?

Because of the large number of errors and omissions that inevitably occur in compiling the balance of payments, a balancing item is included to enable the accounts to sum to zero. In other words, the balancing item is simply an allowance for errors and omissions.

THE FINAL PICTURE

The balance of payments is made up of:

visible balance
+ invisible balance
= balance of payments on current account   (1)
+ net transactions in external assets and liabilities (2)
+ balancing item
= zero   (3)
   (1) + (2) + (3) = 0

Remember that some of the above figures must be negative to obtain a zero balance. Consider the following data for the 1992 balance of payments.

	£m
Visible balance	-13 406
Invisibles balance	4 786
Current balance	-8 620
Net transactions in UK assets and liabilities	8 319
Balancing item	301
	0

The following question on the balance of payments is taken from a UCLES A level paper.

EXTERNAL POSITION OF FOUR SELECTED CARIBBEAN AREA ECONOMIES IN 1988

Small countries such as those in the Caribbean area are very dependent on international trade, since they are unable to produce all that they need. Invariably, their internal development depends upon a particular product or service which is traded with developed economies such as the USA. Many developing economies, including Caribbean countries, are heavily in debt to the governments and financial institutions of richer countries, largely as a consequence of their need to fund the escalating cost of imported energy resources over the last twenty years. The information in the table below shows various aspects of these external economic problems for four Caribbean area economies in 1988. Study this information and answer the questions that follow.

Trade

	External trade as % GDP	Exports to USA as % total exports	Main export
Bahamas	65.1	62.8	Financial services
Barbados	46.0	27.6	Tourism
Jamaica	53.5	45.5	Aluminium
Trinidad & Tobago	36.9	55.3	Petroleum

Balance of Payments, Current Account ($US million)

	Visible exports	Visible imports	Balance of private & official transfers	Balance of all other invisibles
Bahamas	273	1048	-15	671
Barbados	131	458	6	261
Jamaica	833	1228	505	-544
Trinidad & Tobago	1402	1052	-30	-529

Foreign Debt

	Total Debt ($US million)	Total Debt as % GDP	Debt Service Ratio*
Bahamas	195	12.1	3.9
Barbados	746	47.7	11.0
Jamaica	4305	135.2	25.5
Trinidad & Tobago	1994	45.4	9.8

Source: *Vital World Statistics*, Economist Books, 1990 (compilation)

* This shows what proportion of foreign currency earnings from exports have to be devoted to servicing debt repayments.

1 Which country has the most 'open' economy? Explain your answer. (2)

2 a Which country has the largest deficit on its visible balance? (1)
b Calculate the balance of payments on current account for Trinidad and Tobago. (1)
c Give an example of an item you might expect to find in the 'Private and official transfers' section of the balance of payments. (1)

3 a Compare the balance of payments on current account for Jamaica with that for Trinidad and Tobago. (2)
b Suggest reasons for any differences. (3)

4 a Compare the foreign indebtedness of Barbados and Jamaica in 1988. (2)
b State two ways in which the economies of these countries may be affected by significant foreign debt obligations. (2)

5 a From the data provided, identify how these developing countries are economically dependent upon other more developed economies. (2)
b Comment upon the implications of this dependency. (4)

UCLES, June 1993

Exchange rates

An exchange rate is the price of one currency expressed in terms of some other currency. £1 = DM3 would be a typical example.

WHAT DETERMINES A COUNTRY'S EXCHANGE RATE?

Just like any price, an exchange rate is determined by demand and supply. The rate for the pound depends on the number of buyers of sterling, that is the demand, and the number of sellers, that is the supply.

Demand will depend on

- purchasers of UK exports
- investors in the UK
- speculators who expect a rise in the value of the pound.

Supply will depend on

- purchasers of UK imports
- investors abroad
- speculators who expect a fall in the value of the pound.

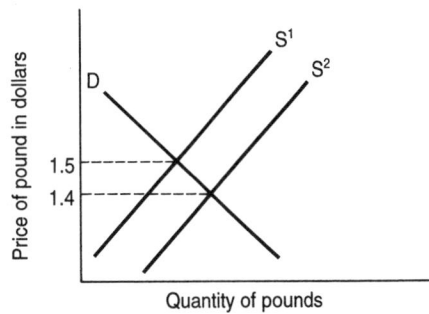

The above diagram shows the pound initially in equilibrium at a rate of £1 = $1.50. D and S^1 are the original demand and supply curves for sterling. However, a fall in UK interest rates has caused a wave of selling of sterling and its value against the dollar has fallen to $1.40. In a currency market free from government regulation the price of the pound will fluctuate continuously as market forces dictate.

THE ECONOMIC EFFECTS OF EXCHANGE RATE MOVEMENTS

When the value of the pound falls, all other factors remaining unchanged, the UK price of foreign imports rises and the foreign price of UK exports falls.

If we assume an exchange rate of £1 = $3, then a bottle of Scotch, costing £10 in the UK, would cost $30 in the USA. If the pound's value were to fall to $2, then the dollar price of Scotch would fall to $20. Similarly, an American-made car costing $30 000 would have a sterling price of £10 000 at a rate of £1 = $3, but would cost £15 000 at £1 = $2.

Thus, it could be expected that a fall in the value of a nation's currency would lead to an increase in the volume of its exports, a decline in the volume of its imports and an overall improvement in its balance of payments. However, these favourable movements in export and import volumes depend upon their elasticities of demand. There would be no point in reducing the dollar price of Scotch if it did not persuade American consumers to drink more. Similarly, increasing the UK price of American cars would serve little purpose if British consumers continued to buy them anyway. If devaluation of the currency is to lead to an improvement in the balance of payments, then this Marshall-Lerner condition must be satisfied:

elasticity of demand for exports + elasticity of demand for imports >1

Note that the above formula ignores the minus sign in the price elasticity of demand.

Furthermore, real life is never as straightforward as economic theory and the above relationship is not always supported by the data. This is because of our old friend *ceteris paribus*. There are a number of factors which can influence a country's trading performance and a deterioration in any one of these could outweigh the competitive advantage gained by currency depreciation.

A fall in a currency might be associated with an increase in domestic inflation. This would mean exports actually rising in price and domestic goods becoming more expensive than imports, thus causing the balance of payments to worsen. It is also possible that non-price factors such as quality and reliability are more important to customers than the price changes brought about by a falling currency.

Other impacts of currency movements could be multiplier effects on the domestic economy, perhaps leading to an increase in employment or even an inflationary spiral.

GOVERNMENT INTERVENTION

The exchange rate is such an important economic variable that governments can rarely resist the temptation to try to manage it in some way. The most extreme form of government intervention is to attempt to maintain totally **fixed exchange rates**. This was the system established by the Bretton Woods conference of 1944, which lasted until 1971.

More recently, the members of the European Union attempted to establish a system of semi-fixed exchange rates, known as the **exchange rate mechanism** or **ERM**. This requires member countries to keep their currencies within certain limits of an agreed rate against the Deutschmark. The UK joined the ERM in October 1990 and sterling had to be kept within a band of 6 per cent either side of £1 = DM2.95. Effectively this meant that it could fluctuate between DM2.77 and DM3.13.

The Bank of England, which is responsible for the external value of the pound, has two instruments which it can use to influence the exchange rate: intervention buying and interest rates.

INTERVENTION BUYING

The Bank of England has a war chest of foreign currencies which it can use to bolster the price of sterling. It simply sells Deutschmarks, for example, and buys pounds, hence increasing the demand for pounds and stabilising its price.

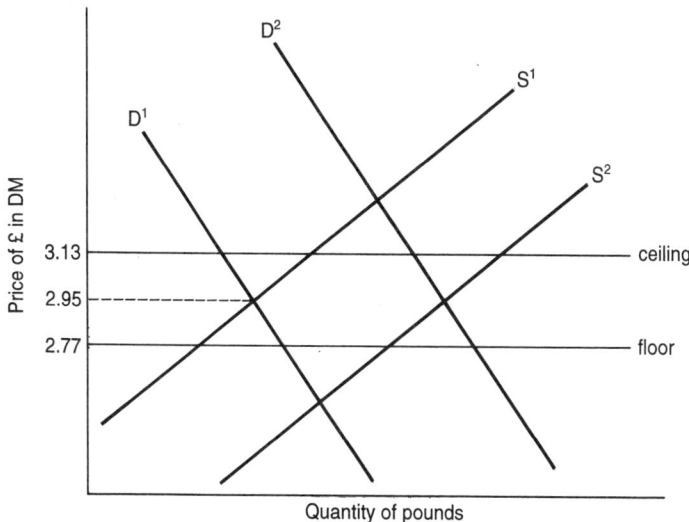

Quantity of pounds

The upper and lower limits of the pound against the Deutschmark

In the above figure, the pound is initially at an exchange rate of £1 = DM2.95. If there were a rise in UK imports from Germany, then there would be an increase in sales of sterling to pay for them, and the supply curve would move from S^1 to S^2. This would cause the exchange rate to fall to £1 = DM2.70. This, however, is below the permitted trading range for sterling and the Bank of England must now intervene to push up the exchange rate. This is achieved by intervention buying of pounds, which moves the demand curve from D^1 to D^2, and the exchange rate is returned to £1 = DM2.95.

In the unlikely event of the pound's value rising above DM3.13, the Bank of England would sell pounds and buy Deutschmarks.

INTEREST RATES

Interest rates are an important determinant of investment flows between countries. All other things being equal, a rational investor will move funds to the country with the highest rate of return. Hence, to prop up the pound against the Deutschmark, the Bank of England should raise interest rates to a level above German rates, thus ensuring a flow of funds from Germany to the UK. Again this increases the demand for sterling and will cause an increase in the exchange rate.

BRITAIN'S DEPARTURE FROM THE ERM

Throughout the summer of 1992 many investors became convinced that the pound's ERM value against the Deutschmark was unsustainable. The high interest rates needed to maintain it were driving Britain deeper and deeper into recession and the government was under great political and economic pressure to change direction. These investors backed their judgement with their money, selling pounds and buying Deutschmarks. Intervention buying by the Bank of England was insufficient to stem the tide of selling pressure, and in September 1992 it bowed to the inevitable, withdrawing sterling from the ERM and allowing it to float. In fact the pound was allowed to sink rather than float as it rapidly descended to around DM2.50 and by January 1995 had reached DM2.25.

Indeed the problems of the ERM did not end with Britain's departure. The remaining members moved to a range of 15 per cent either side of their agreed parity, but even this was not flexible enough to allow for the very different performance of the currencies of the various member states and in March 1995 both Spain and Portugal were forced to devalue. The proposals for a single European currency by the turn of the century look highly unlikely to be achieved.

SPECULATORS MAKE A KILLING

Shrewd financial investors such as George Soros were able to make enormous profits from the events of 1992. The Bank of England, anxious to keep the pound above DM2.77, had to buy pounds at various prices above this ERM floor. Speculators were able to borrow sterling from UK banks and immediately sell it for Deutschmarks at, say, £1 = DM2.80. When the pound fell to DM2.50 they could convert their Deutschmarks back into pounds, repay their loans and keep a healthy profit.

Suppose that on 1 September a shrewd punter borrows £1 million from a London bank and exchanges it for Deutschmarks at £1 = DM2.80. This gives him DM2.8 million. After Black (or White, depending on your point of view) Wednesday he converts his DM2.8 million back into pounds at £1 = DM2.50. He now has £1 120 000. He repays his loan of £1 million and walks away with a profit of £120 000, gained at the expense of the British taxpayer.

THE DECLINE OF STERLING

The pound has been in a state of almost continuous decline since the end of the Second World War. The **sterling trade weighted index** was established in 1975 to measure the pound's value against a 'basket' of 16 other currencies. The relative importance of each currency is based on their percentage of UK trade in manufacturing. This index shows a steady fall in the value of the pound.

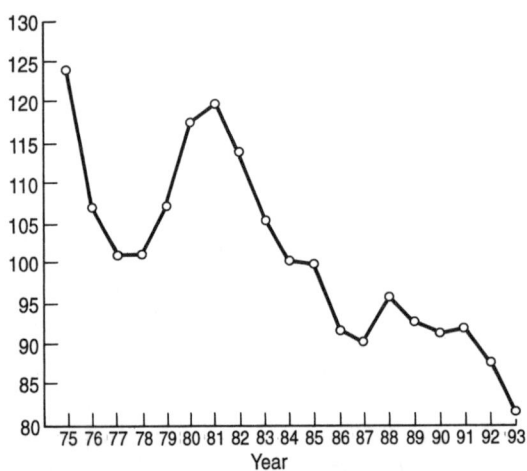

Sterling exchange rate index, 1975–93

At the end of 1973, £1 would have bought DM6.28 or US$2.32. At the end of 1993, the pound was worth DM2.45 or US$1.52; and by February 1995 it had fallen in value to DM2.28.

This depressing performance can be attributed to the relatively high rates of inflation in the UK over the 20-year period in comparison with its trading partners and to generally lower levels of productivity and competitiveness.

The continual fall in the value of the pound since leaving the exchange rate mechanism in 1992 is one of the main reasons why there have been no serious arguments put forward for the pound's rejoining the ERM.

The current debate, which is having severe political repercussions for the government, is whether Britain should sign up for a single European currency. As part of the Maastricht agreement it was planned that a single currency would be in place by 1997.

The economic significance of exchange rates is examined in the following question from a ULEAC A level paper.

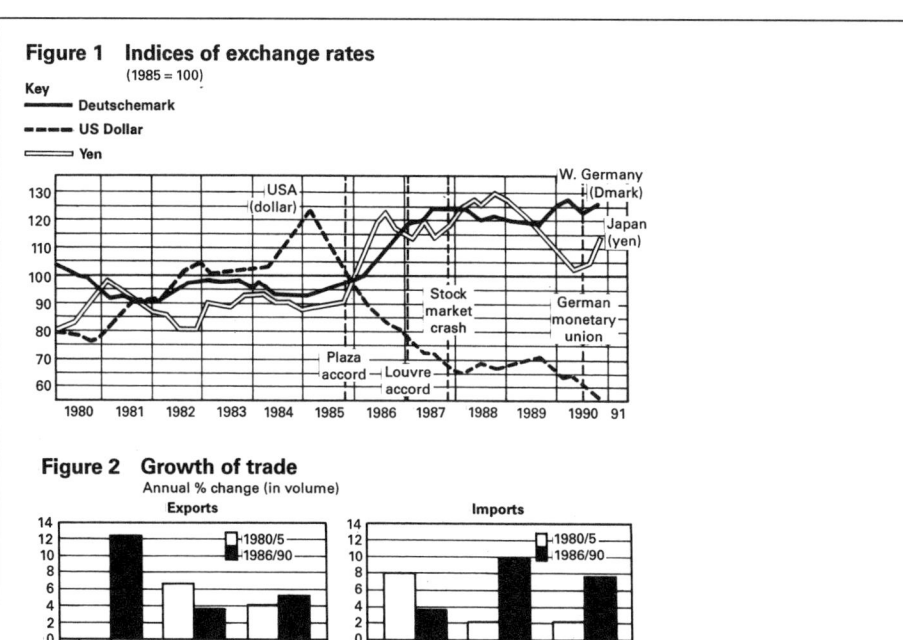

Figure 1 Indices of exchange rates
(1985 = 100)

Figure 2 Growth of trade
Annual % change (in volume)

(Source: M. Wold, 'Japanese responses to changed competitiveness', *The Financial Times*, 17 June 1991.)

1 What does Figure 1 show about the movement of the foreign exchange rate of **a** the Japanese yen and **b** the United States dollar during the period shown? (2)

2 With respect to Japan and the USA, examine how these movements in the foreign exchange rate could explain changes in the volume of exports and imports during the period shown in Figure 2. (8)

3 What other economic effects might these movements in the foreign exchange rate have had on *either* the USA *or* Japan? (6)

4 Despite an appreciation of the German Deutschmark between 1986 and 1991, Germany's exports actually increased. How might this be explained? (4)

Public finance

The term 'public finance' applies both to the ways in which governments raise revenue (taxation) and to the ways in which this money is spent.

This section will look at:

- public expenditure
- taxation
- the public sector borrowing requirement (PSBR).

PUBLIC EXPENDITURE

'Public expenditure' is the term used to refer to how the government spends its (or, more accurately, the taxpayer's) money. The term 'public sector' covers three distinct areas:

- central government
- local government
- public corporations (which include the few remaining nationalised industries such as British Rail and British Coal).

The term 'general government' is used to describe the combined activities of central and local government without the public corporations.

Economists analyse government expenditure in three ways:

- the absolute amount of public spending
- the composition of public spending
- public spending as a percentage of GDP.

THE ABSOLUTE AMOUNT OF PUBLIC SPENDING

Consider the following figures for public expenditure between 1982 and 1992.

Year	Public expenditure (£ billions)
1982	128.8
1983	138.5
1984	147.2
1985	157.8
1986	162.3
1987	169.2
1988	178.2
1989	197.0
1990	215.6
1991	228.3
1992	254.1

The casual observer of these figures can see that between 1982 and 1992 government expenditure almost doubled. However, this was not a consistent trend.

Year	% change on previous year
1983	7.5
1984	6.3
1985	7.2
1986	2.9
1987	4.3
1988	5.3
1989	10.5
1990	9.4
1991	5.9
1992	11.3

The data can usefully be divided into three sections:

- 1983-5 average increase 7 per cent
- 1986-9 average increase 5.8 per cent
- 1990-2 average increase 8.9 per cent.

How can these substantial fluctuations in the rate of growth of public expenditure be explained? The following figures for the rate of **economic growth** in the UK will provide the answer.

During the period 1983-5 the economy was recovering slowly from recession. Real GDP rose at an annual average rate of 3.2 per cent but unemployment lagged behind the rise in output and the government was forced to spend large sums on social welfare benefits.

1986-9 saw the Lawson boom with average growth at 3.8 per cent and unemployment falling to a low of 6.3 per cent in 1989. This allowed the government to cut back on social welfare spending.

Then the 1990-2 period exemplified the old parental adage 'after laughter always tears'. Mr Lawson's boom came to an abrupt end, as did his political career. In 1991/92 economic 'growth' fell to -2.4 per cent and unemployment rose to 9.7 per cent. Government expenditure was in danger of spiralling out of control as social welfare spending escalated.

This inverse relationship between the rate of growth of the economy and the rate of growth of government spending is typical of any automatic stabiliser (see page 64). As aggregate demand falls or stagnates, a compensatory increase in government spending is triggered, thus helping to bring recession to an end.

It also illustrates just how difficult it is for governments to control their own spending. They are at the mercy of economic forces over which they have only limited control. The 1993/94 budget deficit of around £50 billion is clear evidence of this.

THE COMPOSITION OF PUBLIC SPENDING

The second way of analysing government expenditure is to look at how it is distributed among the various government departments. This can vary significantly from year to year, depending on government priorities.

These changing priorities become apparent when we examine the percentages of total spending received by government departments over a period of ten years.

Public spending, by government department, 1982–92

			Percentages
	1982	**1987**	**1992**
Defence	11.2	11.2	9.7
Public services	3.8	3.9	4.9
Public order	3.8	4.4	5.5
Education	11.9	12.3	12.7
Health	10.9	12.4	13.8
Social security	28.3	30.8	33.1
Housing	5.1	5.5	4.3
Transport	3.9	2.4	2.5
Debt interest	10.9	10.6	6.8
Others	10.2	6.5	6.7

- **Defence** The reduction in the priority allocated to defence is the result of the so-called 'peace dividend' arising from the collapse of communism and the ending of the cold war. Western governments feel that the new international order allows them to cut military expenditure and to reallocate resources to other uses.
- **Public services** This section includes the costs of running Parliament, the Inland Revenue and those parts of the civil service not attached to other spending departments. The cost of Parliament was £324 million in 1982 and £871 million in 1992. Readers can make their own judgement on the quality of service that taxpayers have received for their money!
- **Public order** This refers to the police service, the fire service, the law courts and prisons. The substantial increase in expenditure is partly the result of a rise in crime and partly because of large rises in police pay. The cost of the police service rose from £2780 million in 1982 to £7116 million in 1992. This area of spending was analysed in the Sheehy Report (1993), which made a number of recommendations aimed at reducing the cost of running the police.

  An increase in the size of the prison population lies behind the rise in the costs of running the prisons (from £635 million in 1982 to £1726 million in 1992). Here also the government has been attempting to reduce costs through policies such as privatisation and the contracting-out of certain functions to private security firms.
- **Education** Education's share of the 'cake' increased slightly over the ten-year period. This is largely due to demographic trends. Numbers of pupils in primary schools rose from 3.7 million in 1982 to 3.9 million in 1992. Secondary enrolment fell from 4 million in 1982 to 3.1 million in 1992 but is now on an upward trend. Overall pupil numbers are expected to rise until approximately 2002 and to decline significantly thereafter. Numbers in higher education have risen substantially. Educational spending is an area in which the government can hope to make savings in future years.
- **Health** This has been a major growth area for government spending and again the reasons are largely demographic. The proportion of older people in the population is increasing rapidly and with it the need for both hospital and nursing home accommodation.

The elderly as a proportion of total UK population, 1991–2031

Year	Total population	Age group (%) 65+	75+	85+
1991	57.6m	15.8	7	1.6
1996	58.4m	15.8	7.2	1.8
2001	59.2m	15.6	7.5	2.0
2011	60m	16.3	7.5	2.2
2021	60.7m	18.2	8.1	2.3
2031	61.1m	20.7	9.3	2.5

This 'demographic timebomb' has enormous implications for government expenditure. It is the catalyst behind a number of reforms such as

- 'Care in the Community', a policy that aims to keep old people out of expensive nursing home accommodation and instead to be cared for at home
- increasing the age at which women receive the state pension from 60 to 65
- abolishing the state earnings related pension scheme (SERPS).

• **Social security** This is by far the largest single item of government spending. It is also the area in which the government is trying hardest to make cuts. A significant rise in the numbers of people claiming invalidity benefit caused particular concern.

Invalidity benefit, number of claimants, 1981–91

	1981	**1991**
Male claimants	834	1225
Female claimants	249	512
Total	1083	1737

This staggering 60 per cent rise in the overall total of claimants masks an even more staggering rise (129 per cent) in the numbers of long-term (over six months) claimants - from 650 in 1981 to 1490 in 1991.

These figures could only indicate either a substantial deterioration in the health of the nation or widespread abuse of the system. The Secretary of State in 1994, Mr Peter Lilley, believed the latter to be the case and tightened the medical criteria applied to claimants. However, even his draconian measures will make only a small dent in the total social security budget. The recession and the consequential increase in unemployment make inevitable a rise in social security spending and only a return to economic growth will enable the government to trim spending on social security.

It should be clear from this brief review of government expenditure that any major cuts are difficult and painful to achieve. Such cuts involve substantial opportunity costs through the loss of a variety of programmes and services which many would consider to be of great social benefit.

PUBLIC SPENDING AS A PERCENTAGE OF GDP

The third way in which government spending can be measured is to calculate the percentage of GDP which it absorbs. This figure has acquired added significance in recent years with the acceptance amongst policy makers of the idea of **crowding out**. Higher expenditure by the government may involve the transfer of resources from the private sector by means of higher taxes. Alternatively, increases in government spending could be financed by borrowing; in this case the increased PSBR would drive up interest rates, making it too expensive for the private sector to borrow and so reducing private sector investment. Hence a major objective of government policy since 1979 has been to 'roll back the frontiers of the state'.

The following figures illustrate the expansion of government activity in the twentieth century.

General government expenditure as a percentage of GDP, UK, 1891–1992

Year	Government expenditure (%)
1891	10
1911	12
1914–18	35 (average)
1921	25
1931	27
1939	30
1939–45	50 (average)
1945	33
1951	38
1961	35
1971	40
1981	47
1988	39
1992	44

The years prior to the First World War were an era when government limited itself to the delivery of public goods such as defence and law and order. A role in providing merit goods such as education and health care had not yet become politically acceptable. Hence government spending was still a relatively low percentage of GDP.

The First World War, as with all such conflicts, produced a massive increase in the scope of government activity. Britain moved closer to a planned economy as more and more resources were devoted to the war effort.

After the war public expenditure fell back, but not to its pre-war levels. In the 1930s it began to rise again, initially due to the impact of the depression and later because of rearmament.

As would be expected, the Second World War produced a massive rise in government spending, with an average of 50 per cent and a peak of over 60 per cent.

The end of the war brought with it the inevitable reduction in government activity. However, a remarkable change had taken place in the public perception of the appropriate role for government in the economy. There was a determination never to return to the squalor of the depression and a belief that only government action could prevent this. Lord Beveridge, in his famous report, published in 1944, placed responsibility for the creation of full employment firmly on government. Clement Attlee's Labour administration, elected in 1945, founded the Welfare State and nationalised many important industries. The state gradually extended its range of activities in a manner which classical economists would have found unthinkable. All of this had a dramatic impact on the government's share of GDP from 1945 onwards. In 1979, nationalised industries employed 1.5 million people, accounted for 10 per cent of GDP, and dominated large sectors of the economy.

However, this expansion of the public sector failed to produce the golden age sought by Beveridge and others. The performance of nationalised industries was generally felt to be unsatisfactory: costs were high, productivity was low and consumer dissatisfaction was widespread. The electorate was ready for a change of direction.

The election of Mrs Thatcher in 1979 brought to power a government determined to submit the nationalised industries to the discipline of market forces. By the end of 1993, some 47 major companies had been privatised and more than 920 000 jobs transferred to the private sector. For the first time since the Second World War the state's share of GDP started to fall and reached 39 per cent in 1988. The trend did not continue, however, probably due to the impact of the recession. Government spending rose slowly in 1989 and then accelerated as the recession deepened. By the end of 1992 the state's share of GDP had risen to 44 per cent, and was still at this level in 1995/96.

Long-term reductions in the level of government spending will require a radical rethink on what we expect from government. If it is to remain the major provider of health care, education and social security, then substantial reductions are unlikely to be achieved.

TAXATION

The money needed to finance public expenditure is raised by the government through taxation, although this is not the only reason for taxation (see below). Since 1993 the occasion for announcing tax changes has been the November Budget, when tax changes are presented to Parliament along with the government's spending plans.

THE REASONS FOR TAXATION

Taxes are levied for a number of reasons.

- **To finance government spending** This is the oldest and most obvious reason. Some spending may be covered by borrowing (in 1993/94 total government spending was £280.7 billion; £49.8 billion of this was financed by borrowing, the rest was financed by taxation). The danger of relying on borrowing, however, is that it tends to be inflationary.
- **To manage the economy** John Maynard Keynes recommended that the government influence the level of national income through **fiscal policy**. Changes in tax rates could be used to influence macro-economic variables such as the level of inflation, unemployment and the balance of payments.
- **To redistribute income** One of the areas of market failure (see pages 67–71) is the tendency of a free market to result in an unequal distribution of income. Governments may decide to redistribute income to provide for a more equitable distribution. This is achieved by taxing some groups in society and using the money collected from them to increase the income of other groups through welfare benefits.

- **To correct market failures** The price set by the free market often ignores the external benefits and costs of certain kinds of consumption and production. Taxes can be used to influence demand to take account of the failure of the market. Taxes on petrol, for example, are designed to put up the price of petrol and persuade consumers to reduce their purchases in order to reduce air pollution. Sales of newspapers can be encouraged by exempting them from tax.

THE PRINCIPLES OF TAXATION

Taxes by their nature are unpopular, but it is important that the tax system as a whole should be acceptable to individual taxpayers. Look what happened in America in the eighteenth century when the colonists became disenchanted with the system of taxes levied from Westminster!

At the same time as the colonists were revolting over the issue of taxation in America in 1776, Adam Smith was writing about taxation in his book *An Enquiry into the Nature and Causes of the Wealth of Nations*. He put forward four key principles for any system of taxation.

1 **Equity** Taxes should be levied according to the ability of the taxpayer to pay. Taxpayers in similar positions should be treated in the same way.
2 **Economy** The costs of collecting and administering the taxes should be small in relation to the amount collected.
3 **Ease of payment** The means of payment should be convenient to the taxpayer.
4 **Certainty** The amount which is due in tax should be clear and not subject to arbitrary change.

PROGRESSIVE, PROPORTIONAL AND REGRESSIVE TAXES

Taxes can be classified by examining the proportion of income that is paid in tax.

Progressive tax

This is a tax where the proportion of income paid increases as income increases. The marginal rate of tax (that is the percentage of any additional income paid in tax) goes up with income. Income tax in the UK is progressive. This is illustrated in the example below. Bill and Bob are both single; one is a teacher whilst the other is a well-paid head of department.

	Bill	Bob
Total income (£)	32 000	18 000
less Single allowance (tax free) (£)	3 445	3 445
Taxable income (£)	28 555	14 555
Tax payable (£)		
Lower rate of 20% (on first £2500)	500	500
Basic rate of 25% (on the next £21 200)	5 300	3 013.75 (based on remaining taxable income of £12 055)
Top rate of 40% (on remaining £4855 of income) (£)	1 942	
Total tax paid (£)	7 742	3 513.75
% of total income paid in tax	24.2	19.5

In our example, the **marginal rate of tax** increases from 0 per cent for the first £3445 of income to 40 per cent of earnings over £27 145 (£3445 + £2500 + £21 200). The **average rate of taxation** (that is the percentage of total income paid in tax) works out at 24.2 per cent for Bill, and 19.5 per cent for Bob. With a progressive tax, the marginal rate of tax is always greater than the average rate.

Since 1979, however, income tax in the UK has become less progressive as the government has deliberately reduced the proportion of income it takes directly from individuals. This is all part of the **supply-side policies** designed to give incentives to workers in order to persuade them to be more productive and work harder. The table below illustrates the redistributive effects of government on income in the UK.

Redistribution of income through taxes and state benefits, UK, 1991

	Bottom fifth	Second fifth	Middle fifth	Fourth fifth	Top fifth
Total original income (£)	1 570	5 650	13 310	21 100	37 220
Gross income (i.e. income after benefits are added) (£)	5 460	9 170	15 630	22 470	38 110
Disposable income (i.e. income after direct taxes have been deducted) (£)	4 730	7 820	12 830	17 960	29 790

The table shows that before intervention by the government income was very unevenly distributed with the top fifth earning 23.7 times more than the bottom fifth. Benefits closed the difference between top and bottom to a factor of seven, and after income tax the difference was closed further so that the top fifth was earning 6.3 times more than the bottom fifth.

Proportional taxes

This is where the proportion of income paid in tax remains unchanged regardless of the level of income (although the amount of money paid increases). Suppose, for example, there was a tax of 1 per cent imposed on wealth. The actual amount of tax paid would depend on the value of your assets.

Value of assets (£)	Tax paid (£)
1 000	10
10 000	100
100 000	1 000
1 000 000	10 000

Regressive taxes

This is when the proportion of income paid in tax decreases as income increases. The higher paid may pay a larger sum in tax but *as a percentage of total income* it is lower than the percentage paid by those on lower incomes. An example of a regressive tax is the now defunct 'poll tax' or community charge. Expenditure taxes are also often regressive. The following information relating to the imposition of VAT on domestic fuel illustrates the point.

Fuel expenditure of quintile groups of households ranked by disposable income, 1991

	Bottom fifth	Second fifth	Middle fifth	Fourth fifth	Top fifth
Weekly income (£)	120	162.5	240	315	517
Weekly expenditure on fuel (£)	9.47	11.39	12.1	12.7	15.61
VAT at 8% paid per week (£)	0.76	0.91	0.97	1.02	1.25
VAT as % of income	0.63	0.56	0.4	0.32	0.24

Source: Adapted from *Social Trends*, 1993

Even though the *amount* of money spent on fuel and the tax paid *increases* as income increases, the *proportion* of income paid as VAT on fuel *decreases* the higher the household income. This is one of the main arguments used against the trend towards indirect taxes. However, not all indirect taxes are regressive. Those imposed on luxury goods are more likely to result in tax revenue coming from the higher income groups.

Note that any flat rate tax, for example the TV licence, will be regressive in its impact.

DIRECT AND INDIRECT TAXES

There is no unique rule for distinguishing between direct and indirect taxes but the usual textbook definition is that direct taxes are collected directly from the individual or organisation, usually by the Inland Revenue or a local authority; while indirect taxes are taxes on expenditure and collected by some intermediary such as the shopkeeper. Alternatively, direct taxes can be defined as being paid by the person or company on whom the tax is levied; and indirect taxes as being where the incidence of the tax can be passed on.

Since 1979 there have been significant changes in the structure of taxation in the UK. The government has deliberately switched from direct taxes to indirect taxes, as the table below illustrates.

Indirect taxes as a percentage of total tax revenue

Year	%
1978/79	29.3
1979/80	31.6
1980/81	32.4
1981/82	31.4
1982/83	31.6
1983/84	32.6
1984/85	33.5
1985/86	32.6
1986/87	33.7
1987/88	32.9
1988/89	33.5
1989/90	33.1
1990/91	32.8
1991/92	35.6

There have been increases in both the rate of VAT on goods and services and in the number of items covered by VAT. In 1979 the rate of VAT was raised from 8 per cent to 15 per cent. It was further raised to 17.5 per cent in 1991. In 1994 VAT was imposed on domestic fuel and power, albeit at a reduced rate of 8 per cent.

The increases in indirect taxes were necessary to offset reductions in direct taxes. Corporation tax, the tax levied on company profits, was reduced from 52 per cent in 1979 to 33 per cent in 1993.

The reductions in income tax rates have been even more dramatic, as the table below illustrates.

Marginal tax rates (%)

	1978/79	1993/94
Lower rate	25	20
Basic rate	33	25
Higher rates	40 to 83	40
	depending on income level	

In addition to the rates shown in the table, in 1978/79 some income from investment was subject to a surcharge of 15 per cent. This was eliminated in 1979.

The government is now committed to reducing the basic rate of income tax to 20 per cent, although no date has been set for this. It is likely to be financed by increasing the range of goods and services subject to VAT in line with EU tax harmonisation.

WHY CHANGE TO INDIRECT TAXES?

There are various reasons for governments to move towards indirect taxation.

Economic incentives

Supply-side economists argue that indirect taxes are preferable to direct taxes because they create less of a disincentive to work. As direct tax rates increase, work becomes less attractive because the rewards are reduced. By placing greater emphasis on indirect taxes, the tax burden is hidden in the price of goods and can be avoided if workers save rather than spend.

Supply-side economists believe that the output potential of the economy will be raised if workers are permitted to keep the rewards of their efforts. The result is that the aggregate supply curve moves to the right as shown in the diagram. Bottlenecks which cause inflation as demand in the economy grows can then be avoided, and so the economy can achieve inflation-free growth.

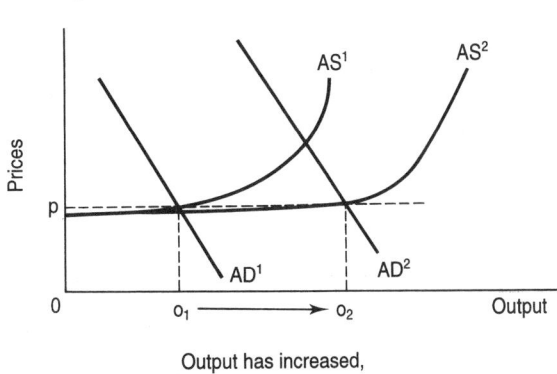

Output has increased, without prices increasing

The effects of a shift towards indirect taxation

There is no clear evidence to support this contention, however. The results of research are ambiguous. Some economists argue that lower income tax rates may actually reduce the incentive to work because the higher disposable income after a tax cut persuades workers to substitute leisure for work (the **income effect** overcomes the **substitution effect**).

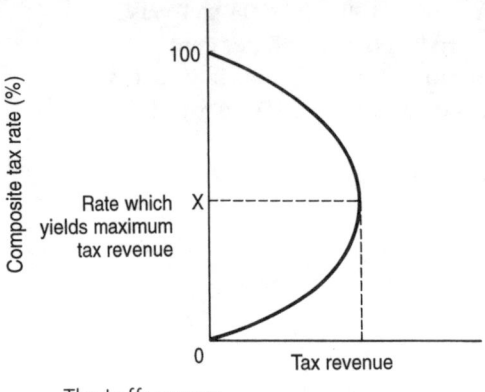

The Laffer curve

Other economists, such as Professor Arthur Laffer, argue that the substitution effect is greater than the income effect and a reduction in income tax rates would encourage effort and lead to an increase in overall tax revenue. His view is presented in a diagram called the **Laffer curve**.

As tax rates are increased, economic activity is discouraged and the rate of growth of tax revenue falls. When the rate reaches OX, an increase in tax rates so discourages economic activity that the total tax revenue falls.

Incentives to save

A shift towards indirect taxes will also provide an incentive to save and use those savings to take entrepreneurial risks. This, allied to tax-free savings plans such as TESSAs (tax exempt special saving accounts), should provide greater funds for investment in the economy and help move the aggregate supply curve to the right.

Cost of tax collection

Indirect taxes are cheaper to administer. Instead of the tax being collected from 22 million taxpayers, indirect taxes are collected from manufacturers and retailers who are far fewer in number. They act as the tax collectors for the government.

Altering demand

The consumption of some goods produces negative externalities which are not included as a cost when the goods are priced in the free market. The government may wish to discourage consumption of such goods in order to reduce the costs to society. Indirect taxes are an effective way of achieving this goal; for example, in 1993, the government committed itself to increasing taxes on fuel in real terms in order to reduce consumption and cut down pollution. The diagrams below show how this is achieved.

(a)

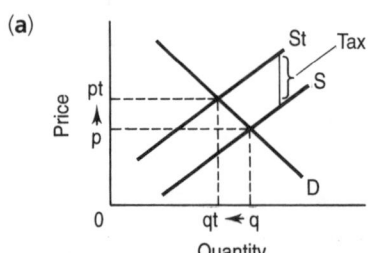

(b)

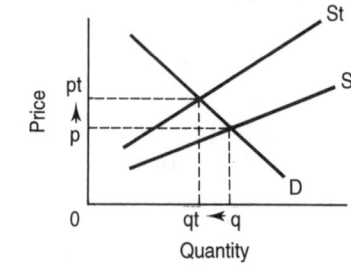

The effect on demand of the imposition of an indirect tax

A tax imposed on a commodity moves the supply curve to the left (from S to St) since it involves an increase in production costs. This raises the price (from p to pt) and, depending on the price elasticity of demand, consumption is reduced (from q to qt). Diagram (a) shows the effect of a **specific tax**, that is a certain amount of money per item; the distance between the two supply curves here shows the tax per commodity. Diagram (b) shows the effect of an **ad valorem tax**, that is a tax based on a percentage of the selling price of the good.

Taxation can be used to achieve both macro- and micro-economic objectives, as shown above, but the main reason for taxation remains the need to finance government spending. As long as there is government, there will be taxation.

THE PUBLIC SECTOR BORROWING REQUIREMENT (PSBR)

If individuals want to spend more than they earn, they either have to draw on their savings or borrow. The same applies to governments. If public spending exceeds revenue from taxes and other sources, the public sector has to become a borrower. The amount which governments borrow to bridge the shortfall between revenue and spending is called the **public sector borrowing requirement** or **PSBR**.

In the UK the PSBR is made up of the borrowing of central government, local government and other state bodies such as public corporations. The table below shows how the size of the PSBR is arrived at. (Note that approximations in each item may make some totals appear inaccurate.)

Determinants of the PSBR in 1993/94 and 1994/95

	£ billion	
	1993/94	**1994/95**
Receipts		
Income tax	57.9	64.4
Corporation tax	14.7	17.6
Value added tax	38.7	43.1
Excise duties	24.7	27.1
Other taxes (e.g. council tax)	38.6	41.2
Social security receipts	39.1	42.8
Other receipts	16.1	16.2
General government receipts	**229.7**	**252.4**
Expenditure		
New control total	244.7	251.3
Cyclical social security	14.0	14.8
Central government debt interest	19.4	22.5
Accounting adjustments	8.0	8.8
General government expenditure excluding privatisation proceeds	**286.1**	**297.3**
Privatisation proceeds	–5.4	–5.5
General government expenditure	280.7	291.8
Expenditure, receipts and borrowing		
General government expenditure	280.7	291.8
General government receipts	229.7	252.4
General government borrowing requirement	51.0	39.4
Public corporations' market and overseas borrowing	–1.2	–1.5
Public sector borrowing requirement	**49.8**	**37.9**

Note: General government comprises central government and local authorities.

(Source: *Economic Briefing*, February 1994)

THE SIZE OF THE PSBR

The size of the PSBR is heavily dependent upon the level of economic activity. During a recession the PSBR would be expected to increase as tax revenues fall due to rising unemployment, falling profits and reduced sales. At the same time government expenditure will automatically increase as there are additional demands upon it to meet benefit claims. Keynes recognised that this would happen and described this effect as an **automatic stabiliser**. As economic activity slowed down there would be an automatic financial injection into the economy which should soften the impact of the recession. The opposite would be the case during a boom.

The table below shows the differing sizes of the PSBR in light of different growth rates. The PSBR in this case is measured as a percentage of GDP.

Variant PSBR projections

	PSBR as per cent of GDP				
	1994/95	1995/96	1996/97	1997/98	1998/99
Central growth assumption	5½	4¼	2¾	1½	¼
Higher growth	5¼	3½	1¾	—	-1½
Lower growth	5¾	4¾	3¾	2¾	2

A HISTORY OF THE PSBR

The chart below shows the history of the PSBR since 1970.

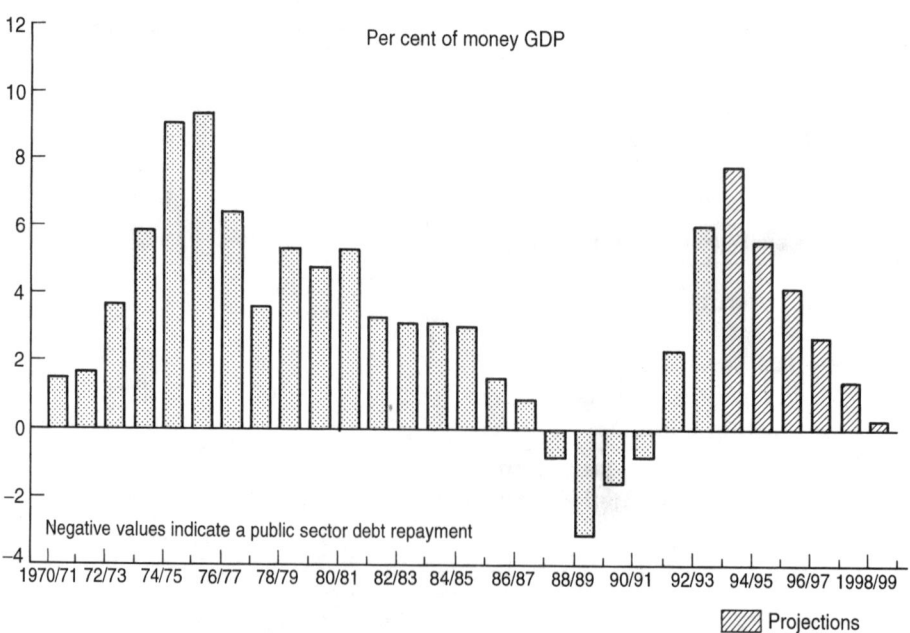

Public sector borrowing requirement, 1970/71–98/99

The recession of the mid-1970s saw the PSBR push up to over 9 per cent of GDP and plunge to under 4 per cent as the Labour government was forced to reduce government spending by the IMF from which it had to borrow money. The recession of the early 1980s saw the PSBR climb to 5 per cent of GDP, but by the time of the 'Lawson boom' at the end of the 1980s the UK government was paying back previous loans rather than borrowing, and for four years there was a PSDR (public sector *debt repayment*). The recession of the early 1990s and the change of prime minister resulted in a less doctrinaire approach to running the economy and, despite the monetarist view that government borrowing stokes inflation by increasing the money supply, the government under John Major incurred a massive PSBR of nearly £50 billion in 1993/94. In the 1994 Budget, however, the chancellor stated that structural reforms and increased growth should ensure that there would be a return to a balanced budget by the end of the decade.

DOES THE PSBR MATTER?

In the 1988 Budget the government committed itself to a balanced budget by 1992. Mrs Thatcher, who often likened the British economy to her father's grocery shop, believed that a country – like an individual – should not live beyond its means. She backed up her homespun economics with the theories put forward by monetarists. They believed that when governments borrowed, the way in which they borrowed could increase the money supply and therefore cause inflation. If inflation was to be kept under control, government borrowing had to be kept down.

Borrowing by the government could hurt the economy in other ways. The sale of government bonds necessary to finance the PSBR can only be achieved by offering a rate of return which would attract people to buy the bonds. This pushes up interest rates in the economy and makes it more difficult for the private sector to invest. This is called 'crowding out' (see page 55).

As interest rates increase, debt interest payments in the future increase. There is the additional effect of higher interest payments on home owners, many of whom may find themselves unable to keep up mortgage repayments. A Conservative government is particularly vulnerable to the political pressures from home owners.

Finally, a high PSBR can weaken the resolve of future governments to take a stand against inflation. An easy way to reduce the burden of past debts is to allow inflation to erode the real value of the national debt, in other words the accumulation of past PSBRs.

The following question from a NICCEA A level paper refers to public spending, tax and the PSBR (see also Question 36 and the model answer provided).

Consider the following passage which relates to Britain's National Debt.

HOW WILL WE FILL THE £50 BILLION HOLE IN OUR POCKET?

The government is planning to borrow £50 billion this fiscal year (1993/4), £1 billion a week or nearly £1000 for every man, woman and child in the country. After allowing for the tax increases in the 1993 Spring Budget, that will fall to £44 billion in 1994/5, £39 billion in 1995/6, £33 billion in 1996/7 and to £30 billion in 1997/8. This level of borrowing is not sustainable.

Kenneth Clarke, the Chancellor, declared last week that he wants to be remembered for guiding British industry through a difficult period, and help 'in my own small way to make a difference to the wealth creating capacity of the nation', but he will fail if he does not take an axe to the budget deficit. In this he needs the full support of the Prime Minister, not the bland (and almost certainly incorrect) assurances that 70% of the deficit is due to the recession.

There are three priorities. The first, and most important, is to allow the economy to grow to its present potential, and to work at raising that potential. If the growth rate rose to 3.5% a year, borrowing would be cut to £10 billion or below, even without any further action on taxation and spending.

A second priority is tax reform. A model tax system was set out by Nigel Lawson in 1984. This would be one in which tax allowances and reliefs are abolished or severely restricted, making room for sharply lower tax rates probably as low as 15% on personal taxation. Present allowances, reliefs and exemptions in Britain's tax system add up to an astonishing £114 billion a year.

A third priority is a radical agenda for public spending. The state's sole concern in welfare, for example, should be to provide a safety net through which the poorest should not be allowed to fall. Britain's blanket system of welfare fails that test. It doles out money to the middle classes, encourages welfare dependency among the poor and still leaves millions in squalor. In 1984 the Treasury, in a green paper on long term spending and taxation, said 'There is an inbuilt tendency for spending to rise, and an inbuilt resistance to expenditure reductions. Without firm control over public spending there can be no prospect of bringing the burden of tax back to tolerable levels.'

If these priorities are implemented they would eliminate the budget deficit, and turn the Tories into a tax cutting party again.

Adapted from *The Sunday Times*, 20 June 1993

1 a What is meant by the National Debt? (2)
b According to the figures given in paragraph 1, by how much will the National Debt have increased by 1997/8? (2)

2 What does the author mean when he says in paragraph 1 that 'this level of borrowing is not sustainable'? (4)

3 In paragraph 2 the Prime Minister claims that 70 per cent of the budget deficit is due to the recession.
a Give four reasons why the budget deficit is likely to rise during a recession. (4)
b According to Keynes how may this budget deficit help reduce the impact of a recession? (3)

4 a Using a diagram, distinguish between an economy growing to its present potential and raising that potential. (paragraph 3) (4)
b Explain two actions which the government could take to help the economy grow to its potential. (4)
c Explain three supply-side measures which may be implemented to raise the potential of the economy. (6)

5 a What would you consider to be the characteristics of a 'good' tax? (3)
b Given the criticisms levelled at the British tax system by the author in paragraph 4, why might many of the taxes in the UK be classed as 'bad' taxes? (2)

6 a Give two examples of benefits which would be included in the 'blanket system of welfare' referred to in paragraph 5. (2)
b What problems might the government encounter in getting 'firm control over public spending'? (4)

Market failure

Most students start their study of economics by examining the basic economic problem of scarcity and choice. We learn that all societies must decide what, how and for whom to produce, and that this is usually called 'allocation' and 'distribution'.

Different societies have evolved different methods of dealing with these issues but the most common method is through the use of **market forces**. In this system the consumer is sovereign and production automatically adjusts to reflect the pattern of consumer demand. This congruence between the decisions of producers and consumers is achieved by what Adam Smith called 'the invisible hand'. Entrepreneurs, in pursuit of profit, will produce only those items which can be sold to the consumers. Hence the market system automatically achieves **allocative efficiency** by producing the goods and services which consumers value most.

The problem of distribution or 'who gets' is resolved equally effectively. Only those who are prepared to pay the market price get the goods and services, and those who can't or won't pay are excluded.

The benefits of such a system are immediately apparent when one compares the achievements of free market economies such as the USA or Hong Kong with those of planned systems such as the former USSR or Albania. The superiority of the free market over state direction is demonstrated by the widespread collapse of communism and the transformation of former communist countries into market economies.

It would, however, be wrong to believe that markets are perfect – there are a number of areas where markets are said to 'fail'. Many data response questions are set on the theme of market failure.

AREAS OF MARKET FAILURE

The main areas of market failure are as follows.

FAILURE TO PRODUCE PUBLIC GOODS

Public goods are those that are collectively enjoyed. Everyone benefits from their provision simply by living in a particular area. It is not possible to exclude anyone from these benefits.

Suppose, for example, a particular area was frequently flooded by very high tides. Could an entrepreneur make a profit by constructing a sea wall? The answer is no, as he or she would be unable to collect payment from the local community. Nothing could be done about 'free riders' who would be quite prepared to enjoy the protection offered by the sea wall but would not be prepared to pay for it. Other examples of public goods are national defence and street lighting.

Since the market cannot provide these vital services, the state must intervene to produce them. It will finance this through taxation.

INSUFFICIENT PROVISION OF MERIT GOODS

Merit goods are those goods that society has deemed to be socially desirable and whose provision it wishes to encourage. If left to the market, such goods would be provided but in limited quantities and distribution would tend to favour the rich.

The most frequently quoted examples of merit goods are education and health care. It would be possible for a profit-seeking entrepreneur to set up a private fee-paying school or hospital but many consumers could not afford these services, while others would not need them. Hence the government steps in to provide education and health care and to distribute it free at the point of use. Indeed, such is the value the state attaches to education that it is not just available but compulsory!

The most important reason for classifying a good as 'meritorious' is the belief that its production and consumption generates significant external benefits for the community as a whole. If a person receives a basic education then not only does the individual benefit, so does society as the quality of the workforce improves. Similarly, medical treatment benefits not only the individual but also society as a whole as epidemics are prevented.

The external benefits of other merit goods, such as sport or the arts, are harder to identify. State sponsorship in these areas is based on a paternalistic view of society. Such activities are felt to be so good for the individual that participation must be encouraged and subsidised.

It is important to remember that the classification of goods as 'meritorious' is a political rather than an economic decision. Different governments have different spending priorities and what is considered to be of great merit by one government may not be by another.

EXCESS PROVISION OF DE-MERIT GOODS

As the name would imply, **de-merit goods** are the opposite of merit goods in that they are felt to be socially undesirable and their production and consumption is discouraged by the government. The most obvious examples of de-merit goods are alcohol, tobacco, pornography (including so-called 'video nasties'), narcotics and prostitution.

The main argument for discouraging, or in some cases banning, these products is that they impose significant external costs upon the rest of the community. Hence the smoker affects others through passive smoking, the use of NHS facilities, and the loss of tax revenue and the payment of benefits when unable to work because of self-imposed illness.

However, external costs are not the only factor in declaring a product to be 'undesirable'. Public morality and paternalism also play a part, so a product may be a de-merit good in one country but not in another. Once again this is as much a political issue as an economic one.

MARKETS IGNORE EXTERNALITIES

When individuals and firms make choices they are motivated by self-interest. The smoker consumes cigarettes without any thought of the wider social implications. Similarly, a firm will attempt to maximise profits and minimise costs without worrying about negative externalities.

A firm may discharge effluent into the atmosphere, causing pollution and great discomfort to neighbours. Since this does not directly affect the firm there is no reason for it to stop, as this would involve extra costs for filters and so on. These costs are effectively borne by the local community and this acts as a kind of subsidy, encouraging the firm to expand production.

Government response to negative externalities

There are many forms of government response to these negative externalities. The most obvious is to 'make the polluter pay' or to **internalise the externality**. This could be achieved by charging the firm for the use of the atmosphere into which it is releasing its effluent. In this way the firm would increase its private costs in line with the social costs, so that a socially optimum use of resources would be achieved. Alternatively, if the firm reduced its pollution, its tax bill would automatically fall.

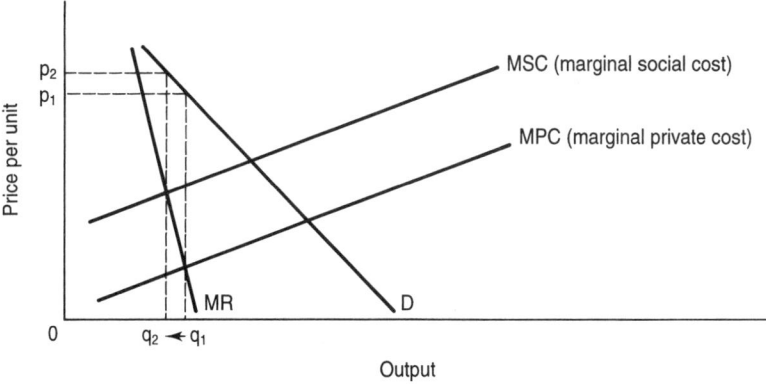

Output

Economic theory states that profits are maximised when marginal cost (MC) equals marginal revenue (MR). In the diagram above, the producer originally equates MR with MPC, leading to output q_1 and price p_1; whereas the correct allocation of resources would involve equating MR with MSC, giving output q_2 and price p_2. The imposition of a tax would have the effect of bringing MPC into line with MSC. This policy will move the supply curve to the left by removing the hidden 'subsidy' that the firm received through making the community pay the costs of its pollution.

Another approach is to prohibit pollution above a certain level and to enforce this with fines or imprisonment.

A major problem with these forms of government action is that not all countries have similar policies. This allows multinational firms to shift 'dirty' production to those states whose environmental policies are least strict. Thus a successful policy to protect the environment would require import controls against such nations. In the absence of such controls environmental protection would probably result in substantial job losses.

The following question from a ULEAC A level paper is on the theme of applying free market policies to the curbing of externalities.

Economics is concerned with the allocation of resources in the face of all opportunities, costs and risks. The market is a mechanism for transmitting dispersed information unknown to any one central planner or computer and providing individuals with incentives to act upon it.

There has been a long tradition of market-based thinking on the economics of the environment. The standard example of an externality is that of the smoking chimney which inflicts costs for which the polluter does not have to pay. The main reason for externalities is not excessive, but inadequate, use of markets and prices. The chimney owner is unrestrained because there is no price to pay for the harm inflicted by his smoke.

The original economic approach was to put a tax on the owner of the chimney and other polluters. The tax can be high enough to impose whatever standard of purification the legislature desires. There is also a case to be made for some combination of taxes for external costs – and subsidies for favourable spillovers. There are other related ideas, such as marketable 'pollution permits'. The more modern approach is to say that adverse externalities arise because property rights have been inadequately defined. It is because no one owns large stretches of the sea that there is an incentive to over-fish.

The principle 'polluter pays' is an attempt to use the property rights approach. This is not always possible, especially where many are involved and transaction costs are heavy. The most obvious example crying out for action is for a 'congestion tax' to be imposed on vehicles coming into busy urban areas.

(Adapted from: S. Brittan, 'The green power of market forces', *The Financial Times*, 4 May 1989.)

1 Explain the meaning of the phrase, 'The main reason for these externalities is not excessive, but inadequate, use of markets and prices' (lines 8–9). (4)

2 Examine and illustrate with a diagram the impact of putting 'a tax on the owner of the chimney and other polluters' (lines 11–12). (6)

3 What policy could a government employ to deal with a situation where it feels that the desirable level of pollution should be *zero*? (2)

4 Analyse the economic effects on firms and households of a 'congestion tax imposed on vehicles coming into busy urban areas' (line 22). (5)

5 With reference to lines 16–18, why does over-fishing occur when property rights are inadequately defined? (3)

THE DEVELOPMENT OF MONOPOLIES

The benefits attributed to market economies are largely dependent upon the existence of high levels of competition. This ensures that consumers are provided with ample choice, that prices are kept down and that firms must produce in the most efficient manner. In the absence of competition it is likely that prices will be higher and output lower than would be the case with competition. Unfortunately, certain industries lend themselves to the creation of barriers to entry and this leads to the development of **monopolies** and **oligopolies**.

Many of the recently privatised public utilities are examples of 'natural monopolies'. Competition in electricity distribution, for example, could only be achieved by allowing the consumer access to power from a variety of different companies. This would entail several power cables being laid down each street in the country, the probable impact of which would be to drive prices up rather than down. In this case the government is content to allow the industry to remain a monopoly and to protect the interests of the consumer by the appointment of a regulator who sets maximum price levels.

In other cases the industry may be referred to the Monopolies and Mergers Commission, who must determine whether a monopoly (defined as 25 per cent of the total market) actually exists and, if it does, determine whether it is 'against the public interest'.

If the Monopolies and Mergers Commission is satisfied that an industry is monopolistic and that it is operating against the public interest, then it may make proposals for the break-up of the monopoly to the Secretary of State for Trade and Industry. This makes the final decision a political rather than an economic one and has led to the criticism that UK competition policy is at best cumbersome and at worst toothless.

MARKETS CREATE INEQUALITIES

In an economy without government intervention the gap in earnings between rich and poor would be enormous. In 1991, the poorest 20 per cent of the UK population would, in the absence of government action, have received an average income of £1570 per annum. The richest 20 per cent would have received £37 220, almost 24 times as much. However, after state intervention in the form of taxation and the payment of benefits, the poorest 20 per cent actually received £4730 and the richest £29 790, or 6.3 times the income of the poor.

No area of government policy has aroused more controversy than the issue of redistribution of wealth. There is a clear conflict between those supply-side economists who believe that incentives and low direct taxation are the key to generating economic growth and those who, on grounds of social justice, advocate higher taxation of the better off.

The debate on issues such as the need for a minimum wage and the UK's opting out of the EU Social Chapter is part of the same conflict between the need for growth and the search for justice.

The following AEB question focuses on this conflict between supply-side and Keynesian economic policies.

SUPPLY-SIDE ECONOMICS: AN ASSESSMENT OF THE AMERICAN EXPERIENCE IN THE 1980s

The supply-side policy in the United States was not designed to secure more revenues for the government or to balance the budget. It was directed toward overcoming the economy's inability to grow without rising inflation and toward reversing the decline in the competitive position of the United States. During the 1970s productivity growth declined sharply. Policy-makers were confronted with worsening 'Phillips curve' trade offs between inflation and unemployment, ending in both rising inflation and unemployment. In 1971 the US merchandise trade deficit turned negative and grew dramatically during the latter part of the decade despite the continuous fall in the dollar exchange rate.

5

10

Keynesian economists could not explain these developments or offer elected policy-makers an escape from the problems. This failure created an opportunity for supply-side economics, which argued that the policy of pumping up demand while neglecting incentives to produce had resulted in stagflation. As incentives were eroded, each additional increment of demand called forth less 15 real output and more inflation. Supply-siders argued that improved incentives and less costs imposed by government would result in greater supply and more efficient use of productive inputs. The supply-side policy is an anti-inflationary one, because its goal is to increase real output relative to demand.

In the Keynesian approach, a fiscal change operates to alter demand in the 20 economy. A tax rate reduction, for example, raises the disposable income of consumers. With government spending held constant, the increased consumer spending stimulates supply and moves the economy to higher levels of employment and gross national product. In this view, the size of the deficit determines the amount of the stimulus. 25

In contrast, supply-side economics emphasises that fiscal policy works by changing relative prices or incentives. High income tax rates and regulation are seen as disincentives to work and production regardless of the level of demand. As people respond to the higher after tax income and wealth, or greater profitability, incomes rise and the tax base grows, thus feeding back 30 some of the lost revenues to the Treasury. The saving rate also rises, providing more funds for government and private borrowing.

(Source: *Extracted from an article by Paul Craig Roberts in the National Westminster Bank Quarterly Review February 1989*)

1 What is meant by the following:
  a 'to balance the budget' (line 2)   (2)
  b 'worsening "Phillips curve" trade offs between inflation and unemployment' (lines 6 and 7)?   (4)

2 Explain why the writer argues that 'supply-side policy is an anti-inflationary one, because its goal is to increase real output relative to demand' (lines 18 and 19).   (3)

3 Examine the view put forward by some supply-side economists that a cut in tax rates will not necessarily result in a fall in tax revenue.   (6)

4 Contrast Keynesian and supply-side economists' views of the way in which fiscal policy might be used to influence the level of national output and employment.   (10)

AEB, June 1991

Chapter 3

Data response questions

Approaching the question

When answering data response questions there are a number of important points to remember.

- **Look at the mark allocation** This will give you an idea of the importance attached to each question and the length of time you should spend on it. A common complaint from examiners is that students give lengthy answers to questions which they could have (and in some cases did) answer in the first two lines of their response.
- **Read through the data carefully** and make sure you understand what is shown on a table or graph, or the main argument in a passage.
- Take time to **relate the questions asked to the data given**. Sometimes an examiner will direct you to a particular table, graph or paragraph. In other cases you may be left to sift through the data to obtain the relevant information for yourself. It is sometimes helpful to underline or annotate the data that you feel is going to be of use in answering a particular question.
- **Use the data** Where there are figures or other information to back up your answer, make sure you use them and quote them in your answer. Almost every chief examiner complains about the failure of students to use the data given in questions. The whole point of data response questions is to test your ability to apply data to economic principles.
- **Apply your knowledge** Think about how economic principles and concepts can be applied to the data in a question.
- Where a question involves the use of a chart or graph, be sure that you **look at the scale** and **read any footnotes** carefully.
- **Do not be put off by statistics** Many students find statistical data difficult to deal with. However, remember that at A level students are not required to do difficult manipulations with statistics. At most, simple calculations of percentage changes or examinations of trends is all that is required (see chapter 1 of this book).

APPROACHING DIFFERENT TYPES OF DATA

It is useful to examine how different types of data should be approached and the kind of responses you could give to each type. You are most likely to be faced with time-series data, cross-sectional data and textual information.

TIME-SERIES DATA

This is the term used to refer to data that show what has happened to *an economic variable over a period of time*. The most common examples are unemployment statistics, national income statistics and figures for international trade. Questions usually require you to explain what has happened to a particular economic variable over time. The examiner is interested in your ability to identify trends in the data.

The one thing to avoid is a running commentary on the figures, simply giving the examiner a re-run of the statistics in words. Try instead to *analyse* the figures in some or all of the following ways.

- **Look for a trend** or trends, since there may be a number of distinct paths followed by the figures over the period in question.

- **Highlight any marked deviations** from the general trend.
- **Show the range** of the figures. For example, if you are examining unemployment rates over a period, what was the highest and the lowest rate? The difference will give you the range.
- **Calculate an average** over the period and compare the figures showing the years which were higher or lower than the average.
- **Plot the figures on a rough graph** to illustrate the trends, if this is appropriate.
- **Look at changes** in figures in terms of *percentage* change as well as *absolute* change.

Example

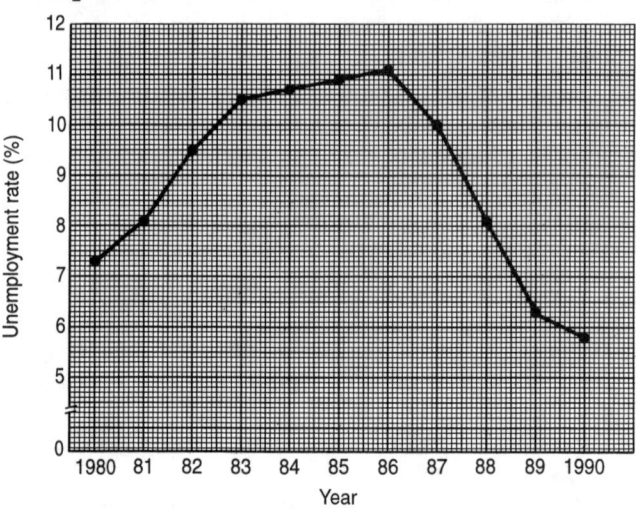

Unemployment in the UK, 1980–90

A typical question may ask you to explain what happened to unemployment in the UK over the decade of the 1980s. A good answer would highlight the following points.

a There are two distinct trends shown. From 1980 to 1986 the unemployment rate rose from 7.3 per cent to 11.1 per cent. Since 1986 there was a steady reduction in the unemployment rate from 11.1 per cent to 5.8 per cent.
b The unemployment rate varied from 5.8 per cent to 11.1 per cent, giving a range of 5.3 per cent.
c The average unemployment rate for the decade was 8.9 per cent. The first two years of the decade and the last three years showed rates below the average.

The amount of detail you give in your answer will depend upon the marks allocated. If the question carried two marks you would gain total marks by covering point **a**, *but make sure you quote the data*. It is not enough to say 'Unemployment rose between 1980 and 1986 and fell between 1987 and 1990.' This superficial type of answer is criticised every year by examiners.

CROSS-SECTIONAL DATA

Cross-sectional data relates to *a number of economic variables*. It may be given over a period of time or for a number of different economies or groups. The main point of questions based on this type of information is to identify relationships between economic variables and to use economic theory to explain how and why variables may be related.

The important points to look out for with data of this nature are as follows.

- **Identify any relationships** between the data if there are any. It may well be that the two variables are totally unrelated. A knowledge of economic theory can be important here since it will help you identify relationships which may occur, for example between interest rates and investment (the marginal efficiency of capital theory).
- **Be aware of time lags** If there is no immediate relationship evident, don't write off the possibility – look more carefully. There may be a *time lag* between one variable changing and the effect it has on other variables, for example the money supply and inflation.
- **Use your knowledge of economics** The data will not give you the cause of any relationship. You need to know the economic theory behind the data to enable you to identify a relationship. Once you have done this, try to explain the relationship in terms of the theory you have learnt. Remember, it is not true that data response papers require no revision! Your knowledge of economic theory and concepts is all important.

Example

Pattern of UK household expenditure, 1989

Percentage of reported expenditure on categories of spending

Average weekly income	Food	Housing	Fuel, light and power	Alcohol	Tobacco	Transport and vehicles	Clothing	Household goods and services	Misc
Under £60	27.3	14.1	13	3.7	4.3	6.8	5.2	12.5	13.1
£200 to £250	20.5	19.5	5.6	4.7	2.8	14.8	6.2	10.9	15
£525 and over	15.8	16.4	3.1	4.5	1.2	18.3	7.9	12.1	20.7

A typical question based on this data might be 'Identify and comment upon the main trends in the data and explain whether or not they are consistent with economic theory.' A good answer would cover the following points.

a There is a clear relationship between spending patterns and average household income. The lower the average income the greater the percentage of income spent on necessities such as food and fuel. For the income ranges given, the percentage of income spent on food falls from 27.3 per cent to 15.8 per cent and for fuel the percentage of income spent falls from 13 per cent to 3.1 per cent. (Note that this does not mean that the better off you are the less you spend on these items. Richer households may spend more money on food and fuel, but it is a smaller *percentage* of total income. This is a common mistake made by students.)

b As households become richer a greater percentage of income is spent on transport, which rises from 6.8 per cent to 18.3 per cent, and clothing, which rises from 5.2 per cent to 7.9 per cent. (Notice that there is no need to use every figure given in the table. Select the information that helps illustrate the most important relationships.)

c Economic theory can be used to explain the relationships identified. Some goods have a high income elasticity, whilst others have a low or even negative income elasticity. Food tends to have a low or negative elasticity and this would explain why the percentage of income spent on food actually falls as income increases. On the other hand, transport has a high income elasticity, especially private transport, therefore it would be expected that as income increased a greater proportion would be devoted to what can be classed as a luxury item.

d A good answer would also identify factors other than income which would affect spending. For example, lower income households tend to be made up of older people which may in turn explain the lesser importance of expenditure on clothing or housing in these households.

Cross-sectional data in particular highlights the need for a good thorough knowledge of economic theory.

TEXTUAL INFORMATION

Most examination boards now include one textual question, or a question with a table or graph backed up by text.

Remember to read through the whole passage first and then try to relate parts of the passage to the questions asked. Don't be afraid to mark on the paper any parts which you feel are relevant to a particular question. You may find it helpful to make notes in the margin or underline parts of the text.

Often the questions asked will be a mixture of those based on the text and those requiring you to apply your own knowledge of economic principles to the theme contained in the text.

CONCLUSION

The more you know about the subject of the data, the easier the questions will be. With this in mind, as part of your preparation for the data response paper and indeed throughout your A level course, make a point of keeping up to date with world events through regular reading of quality newspapers and appropriate journals. Data response questions often assume a certain amount of knowledge of current affairs as well as knowledge of economics.

Given the variety of data response questions, there can be no set approach to answering them. Some questions will require very specific answers, while other open-ended questions leave you to decide what information is required.

Whatever the question, however, there are a few rules to remember.

- Always quote data to back up your answers. Do not give vague replies.
- Your answers should be more than paraphrases of the data, they must *interpret* and *analyse* it.
- Apply basic economic theory to appropriate situations and questions.
- Select the data which helps you justify your answer.
- Make sure your answer has a structure to it and follows a logical sequence. This is especially important with the more open-ended questions which carry a high number of marks. Some of these require answers in the form of mini-essays.

The questions in this book will give you practice with both specific and open-ended questions; they also give you plenty of opportunity to apply each of the above principles.

Market system v. planned system

The fever of liberation

The eye is a better guide to the new reality of rural life in post-collectivisation Albania than the dry and inadequate statistics. But, for the record, the IMF estimates that agricultural output rose by 14 per cent last year and forecasts another 8 per cent gain this year.

A sceptical attitude to the statistics is merited above all by the sheer scale of the changes which have taken place following the decrees abolishing collective farms three years ago and the redistribution of their lands to nearly half a million peasant farmers with an average holding of 1.4 hectares.

Decollectivisation was followed by an orgy of looting as the new landowners scavenged for materials with which to build primitive chicken coops, pig sties and storage space. The avidity of the search for building materials coincided with relief at the end of an absurd agricultural system. The former regime drove the entire nation to near starvation by banning private rearing of animals of any kind.

Three years later the rural towns have taken on a new liveliness. On the fertile coastal plains the fields, divided into small strips, are full of hardworking women cropping wheat and alfalfa with scythes. On the reclaimed marshland closer to the sea many of the fields of the former state farms remain large and wheat is being cut by combine harvesters.

With bread prices at world market levels following the removal of subsidies last July, farmers are getting ready to sell surplus grain to the state or private traders. Politically and economically, fulfilment of the never honoured Leninist slogan 'land to the peasants, bread to the workers' has been the determining factor in the success of post-communist stabilisation policies.

Allowing peasants to grow their own corn, bake their own bread, raise livestock and grow crops for their own consumption and sale has relieved the government of its inherited obligation to provide bread and basic foods. On the demand side, the elimination of subsidies, compensated for by higher wages, has drastically reduced the demand for bread, which was often thrown away or latterly fed to cattle when sold at the old subsidised price.

The last three years have proved that a return to virtually medieval strip farming and free markets is more productive than enforced collectivisation. The future of agriculture now lies in a consolidation of strips into larger units once peasants are permitted to buy and sell land.

(Source: Adapted from *The Financial Times*, 21 July 1994)

Read the above passage and then answer the following questions.

1 Referring to paragraph 1, why may economic statistics often prove inadequate? (3)

2 What is meant by the term 'collective farms' in paragraph 2? (1)

3 Give three benefits of the move away from collectivisation to a free market system. (3)

4 What does the Leninist slogan in paragraph 5 mean? Explain why a collectivist regime might have problems in achieving this ideal. (5)

5 With the aid of a supply and demand diagram, explain why the waste referred to in paragraph 6 might have arisen, and how the abolition of subsidies and the new free market freedoms of producers could help eliminate waste. (5)

6 What disadvantages might Albania experience as a result of the market reforms? (3)

The priceless countryside
The recreational benefits of environmental goods

Some recreational facilities are priced in the market place like normal economic goods. However, many forms of recreation in the countryside and associated with environmental attributes are not priced by the market. Some conservationists regard parts of the countryside as priceless, of infinite value, which should be preserved at all costs. Some features are undoubtedly unique, but for most recreational sites there is a maximum that people are willing to pay for their use and preservation.

The countryside and some environmental assets are priceless in the sense of not being priced by the market. They are not priced because it is impossible or infeasible to charge visitors for their use. It is impossible, for example, to exclude the public from drives in the countryside or from historic cities such as York.

It is important to price and value the countryside. A priceless countryside may mean that insufficient land and resources are devoted to recreational provision and associated environmental protection. The countryside is the emblem of environmental conservation. Groups concerned with rural conservation and enjoyment of the countryside are flourishing and expanding.

Table 1 *Growth in Membership of Voluntary Conservation and Countryside Recreation Organisations*

	1968/69	1978/79	1988
National Trust	176,900	780,000	1,663,552
Royal Society for the Protection of Birds (RSPB)	37,748	250,765	442,140
County Wildlife Trusts	35,087	128,944	204,776
Ramblers' Association	17,193	29,017	62,861
British Trust for Conservation Volunteers	1,300	10,000	60,000
Council for the Protection of Rural England	15,000	28,000	36,000

Source: Countryside Staff Training Advisory Group (1989). *Training for Tomorrow*

The growth in membership of recreational and environmental organisations (see Table 1), is mirrored by the growth of visits to the countryside. The total number of countryside visits in an average summer month is estimated to be between 80 and 100 million, the majority to non-priced sites. This would suggest that the countryside forms an extremely valuable but unpriced resource.

The countryside is characterised by the 'public good' nature of many of its environmental attributes, which are not priced by the market. The 'public good' nature of much countryside recreation invariably means that financial revenue is not an adequate indication of the benefits of these facilities. This inevitably requires some form of public intervention, typically a public subsidy.

Payments to farmers in Environmentally Sensitive Areas maintain particular habitats, such as the grazing marshes which are regarded as a feature of the Norfolk Broads. Only by valuing these landscapes and environmental benefits can we be sure that subsidies are being efficiently spent.

In other instances, charging for countryside recreation and access to unspoilt natural wonders may also ensure that they survive. Nature tourism holds the promise of providing developing countries with both funds and incentives to boost conservation efforts. Pricing will simultaneously control the number of tourists while collecting enough funds to improve the management of protected areas. Good economics is good ecology.

(Source: Adapted from the *Royal Bank of Scotland Review*, no. 172, December 1991)

Read the passage and then answer the following questions.

1 Give two examples of recreational facilities which are priced in the market place. (2)

2 a Give an example of a recreational facility which is not priced in the market place. (1)
b Why are many recreational facilities difficult to price? (3)
c Why is it important to price and value that part of the countryside used for recreation? Explain your answer. (4)

3 a Table 1 shows the growth of voluntary conservation and recreation organisations between 1968 and 1988. Describe the relative growth of each of the organisations. (5)
b What factors might explain the growth recorded in the table? (4)

4 a Why may the revenue obtained from those who use the countryside not cover the costs of providing it? (2)
b List three ways in which the government might intervene to protect a natural habitat. (3)

5 Explain the concluding sentence of the article. (5)

Demand and supply

Good news from the Woolwich

Home owners yesterday (8/8/94) received a mid-summer fillip from the Woolwich Building Society. Donald Kirkham, the group chief executive, described the housing market as showing a 'gradual slow improvement' and predicted that house prices should rise by 3% this year with the number of transactions set to rise by 7%.

These figures indicate strong demand for housing as they came 'in spite of significant tax increases and a reduction in <u>mortgage interest tax relief</u>'.

Martin Ellis, the Woolwich's economist, explained what lay behind this mood of confidence on the part of buyers: 'Prospective borrowers are more confident that the economy is improving as they see unemployment falling and more home owners coming out of the <u>negative equity trap</u>. At the same time homes are still affordable and mortgage rates remain low.'

The Woolwich can now look forward to more profitable times after a period of slow trading during which the housing market was stagnant. Demand for mortgages was low and this reduced sales of such highly profitable by-products as insurance and PEPs.

However, every cloud has a silver lining and the Woolwich may have been quite pleased to see this fall in mortgage applications as it coincided with a substantial fall in net investment from savers. In the first 6 months of 1994, deposits fell from £398m to a mere £22m as savers sought out more profitable homes for their money.

Mr Ellis said, 'People have been investing in equities and unit trusts rather than in building societies.'

The low level of mortgage demand removed the need for the Woolwich to borrow from other financial institutions.

---

1 Use demand and supply analysis to explain the changes in the housing market described in paragraph 1. (5)

2 What factors gave rise to the changes referred to in question1? (4)

3 Explain the terms
 a 'mortgage interest tax relief' and
 b 'negative equity trap'. (6)

4 Why has the Woolwich found it difficult to attract funds from savers? (5)

Free market to defeat drug barons

The government policy of increasing the penalties for possession of drugs has recently been attacked by those whose job it is to enforce this legislation.

Mr Mike Bennett, chairman of the London Police Federation, said: 'Just to announce a fivefold increase in the fine, instead of looking at the problem, won't make it go away.'

One person who has looked at the problem from an economic perspective is the well-known free market economist, Professor Milton Friedman. He argues that the root cause of the so-called drugs problem is the policy of prohibition. Just like the banning of alcohol in the USA in the 1920s, it has created far more problems than it has solved. Then as now it has led to the rise of gangsters who have made vast profits by controlling the distribution of a product for which there is a ready market and a limited supply.

Friedman contends that prohibition has led directly to:

- the invention of 'crack' as a cheap substitute for cocaine whose price was made artificially high by its illegality
- the ghettoes in American cities falling under the control of drug barons
- South American countries such as Colombia, Bolivia and Peru having to wage wars of attrition against well-entrenched drugs' cartels, a situation which Friedman designates as one of 'narco-terror'.

Professor Friedman argues that the social cost argument for banning drugs simply does not hold water. Drug related crime would be substantially reduced by legalisation. Criminal gangs would not fight for control of the distribution of a product whose market price had fallen to barely profitable levels. Drug users would be much less likely to damage their health by the use of dirty needles and impure narcotics, and there is little evidence of any substantial increase in drug use from those countries, such as Holland, where legalisation has been tried.

---

1 What does the writer mean by referring to Friedman as a 'free market economist'? (4)

2 Use demand and supply analysis to describe the probable impact of 'decriminalisation' on the market for drugs. (6)

3 Drugs are often described as de-merit goods. Name two other de-merit goods and explain why they are described as such. (6)

4 Describe two policies, apart from a complete ban, which a government could use in dealing with de-merit goods. (4)

Platinum oversupply forecast to continue

Western platinum supply this year will be well ahead of demand, according to Johnson Matthey, the world's biggest platinum marketing group. Platinum's price during the next six months is likely to range between US$350 and $390 a troy ounce, as long as there is no market disturbing news from South Africa or Russia, the two biggest producing countries.

The platinum market, unlike many western base metals markets, is no longer in turmoil because of Russian exports. However, South African producers have little room left for further voluntary closures of capacity. It is difficult for the mines to forego revenue by reducing shipments. South African producers will continue to increase output until 1997 when their present expansion programmes are scheduled to be completed. If this aggravates market oversupply and causes further price weakness, the mines with the highest costs may not avoid closure or sale.

Johnson Matthey predicts that platinum demand will grow by 6 per cent this year, thanks to increased consumption by the automative and jewellery industries. Automative demand will rise by 12 per cent, driven by the European Commission's regulations (which have required anti-pollution catalysts to be fitted to more cars) as well as higher car production on the American continent. Platinum supply is forecast to grow by 10 per cent, with South African platinum shipments up by 18 per cent and representing 77 per cent of total supply.

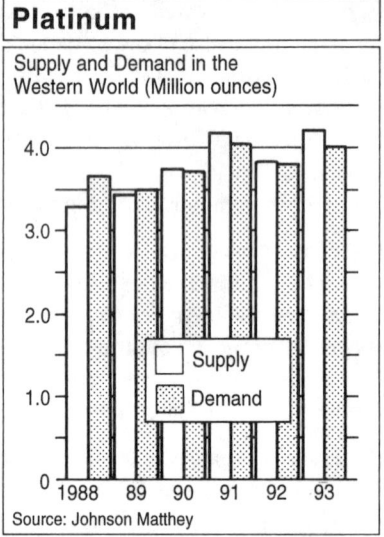

Platinum

Supply and Demand in the Western World (Million ounces)

Source: Johnson Matthey

(Source: Adapted from *The Financial Times*, 17 November 1993)

1 a Using the diagram, describe what happened to the demand and supply of platinum between 1988 and 1993. (3)
b Draw a demand and supply diagram to illustrate the market situation in 1993. (3)
c From the information given about the demand and supply of platinum, what would you expect to have happened to the price of platinum during the period 1988–93? (4)

2 List the factors that determine the demand for platinum. (4)

3 a What is meant by elasticity of supply? (2)
b From the information contained in paragraph 2, would you describe the supply of platinum as elastic or inelastic? Explain your answer. (It may be helpful to think about the short term and the long term.) (6)

4 What kind of market structure would you describe the platinum market as having? Use the information in the passage to justify your answer. (3)

Spanish hotels to lift prices by 20%

British tour operators, currently booking hotel space for 1995, are resisting plans by Spanish hoteliers to raise prices by 20 per cent.

Cosmos, which takes 250,000 people to Spain every summer, says a rise of 5 per cent would be acceptable. Richard Prosser, Cosmos's product director, said Spain could price itself out of the market. 'The industry estimates that demand drops by roughly 1 per cent every time the cost of a holiday increases by 3 per cent.'

Mr Prosser said a good example of price rises backfiring was in Cyprus, which in 1992 had an extremely good year, but then put its prices up by between 30 and 50 per cent and drove tourists away.

Thompson, the biggest tour operator in Britain, is taking legal action against hoteliers who have 'gazumped' hundreds of Britons by selling their prebooked rooms to German and Scandinavian tourists at higher rates.

Operators have said that sudden rises in the cost of Spanish holidays could mean holiday-makers switch to Greece or Cyprus next year.

The Spaniards, however, believe that room rates have been kept low for too long and increases are necessary to enable them to invest in and upgrade their properties.

A spokeswoman for the Spanish tourist office said rises of 15 per cent were 'absolutely reasonable'. She said, 'Prices have not risen since last year and the peseta has been devalued. Britain is now coming out of recession and the question of price should be less important than that of quality. We have asked hoteliers to be reasonable in their demands.'

(Source: Adapted from *The Times*, 11 June 1994)

1 Identify two pieces of evidence from the passage which would indicate a rise in demand for Spanish hotel rooms. (4)

2 What do you think is the most important reason for this rise? (2)

3 Define the term 'price elasticity of demand'. (1)

4 Use the information in paragraph 2 to calculate the price elasticity of demand for a holiday in Spain. (2)

5 Why do you think demand for Spanish holidays is likely to be less elastic than demand for holidays in Cyprus? (2)

6 If Spanish hoteliers did push up prices by 20 per cent, how would this affect demand for rooms? (2)

7 Explain the term 'gazumped' in paragraph 4. (2)

8 Describe with a numerical example how a devaluation of the peseta against the pound would affect the demand by UK tourists for holidays in Spain. (5)

Cut-price Sun claims first blood in war on tabloids

Newspaper groups have only slowly accepted that the decline in circulation among the tabloid dailies is more than a short-term phenomenon. At first it was blamed on the recession and rising unemployment, but executives at Wapping, including the editor of the *Sun*, believe one of the fundamental reasons the tabloid market has fallen from daily sales of 12.8m in June 1983 to 10.6m in June 1993 was the sharp rise in the price of newspapers over the decade of an average 11% per year.

Their belief that price sensitivity was the key to steady decline in the market was bolstered by diverse factors. They argued that the *Daily Mirror*'s decision to raise its cover price last July by 2p to 27p (the *Sun* stayed at 25p) had been met by market resistance. A test cut-price campaign in May provided conclusive evidence that price reductions would boost sales considerably.

There had been heated speculation in the newspaper industry that the *Sun*, part of News International, was to launch a price war. The speculation became reality when on Monday 28th June 1993 the *Sun* decided to break the mould and drop its price by 20% to 20p, 7p cheaper than the *Mirror*.

Rupert Murdoch, chairman of News International, had been increasingly convinced that unless something dramatic was done, the slide in the *Sun*'s circulation would continue indefinitely. The test cut-price campaign in May seemed to support the idea that a lower price would result in higher circulation and, eventually, higher rather than lower revenues.

The move came at a particularly serious time for the Mirror Group. For months it had been grooming itself to float the 54% stake owned by the late Robert Maxwell. A price war is bad news in any industry, but for a group struggling with the problems left by the Maxwell collapse it was potentially disastrous. The move also came at a bad time for the third big newspaper group United Newspapers, which publishes the *Daily Star* and *Express* titles, which was raising £191m by a rights issue.

David Montgomery, the Chief Executive of the Mirror Group, knew he had to respond decisively. He cut the price of the *Daily Mirror* for one day only by a dramatic 17p. It cost the Mirror Group an estimated £500,000, and the share price dropped by 20p, but he reckoned it would confuse the market, divert attention from the *Sun*, attract new readers to the *Daily Mirror* and would be cheaper than matching the *Sun* penny for penny.

It seemed Montgomery's one-off strike worked. The *Daily Mirror* sales, which soared more than 500,000 on Monday, ended the week unchanged from the previous week. The *Sun* with heavy promotions gained 200,000 daily sales but not at his expense. The *Sun* had also proved the point that a lower price would stimulate demand.

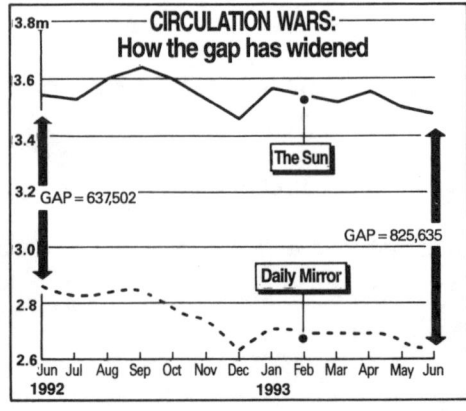

CIRCULATION WARS: How the gap has widened

The Sun

GAP = 637,502

GAP = 825,635

Daily Mirror

Jun Jul Aug Sep Oct Nov Dec Jan Feb Mar Apr May Jun
1992 1993

(Source: Adapted from *The Sunday Times*, 18 July 1993)

1 a What happened to the sales of daily newspapers over the decade 1983–93? (1)
b List four factors which could have caused the fall in the demand for daily newspapers. (4)
c From the information given in paragraph 1, would you describe the demand for newspapers as price elastic or price inelastic? Show your calculations. (4)

2 From the information given in the passage, what kind of market structure does the newspaper industry have? Explain your answer. (2)

3 a Using the diagram, describe what happened to the gap in sales between the *Daily Mirror* and the *Sun* between June 1992 and June 1993. (2)
b What factors could explain the changes in the sales gap between the two papers over the period shown? (2)
c Using the information in paragraph 2 and the sales information in the diagram, calculate the cross-elasticity of demand for the *Sun* with respect to the *Daily Mirror*. (Compare the sales figures for July 1992 with those of September 1992.) (4)
d What does your answer to the cross-elasticity of demand calculation indicate about the relationship between the *Sun* and the *Mirror*? (2)

4 Using the diagram and the sales for the day after the price cuts in the *Sun* (recorded in paragraph 7), state whether the conclusion underlined in paragraph 4 was correct. (Show your calculations.) (3)

5 a What evidence is there for the sentence underlined in paragraph 5? (3)
b If price wars are so disastrous, in what other ways could newspapers compete? (3)

NICCEA, 1994, paper 3

Industrial economics

Eurotunnel starts battle for customers

Table 1

Eurotunnel's revenue forecasts, £m				
Date of forecast	Year to which forecast applied			
	1993	1994	1995	1996
1987	488	762	835	908
1990	393	764	833	904
1993	—	224	554	691

Table 2

Breakdown of the cross-Channel market in 1996				
TOTAL MARKET 16M CAR PASSENGERS				
Company	Journey time	Market share	Market share (now)*	Current price
Stena Sealink	**75 mins**	**15%**	30%	**£126–320**
Hoverspeed	**35 mins**	**3%**	6%	**£142–338**
P&O	**75 mins**	**32%**	64%	**£139–320**
Eurotunnel	**35 mins**	**50%**	0%	**£220–310**

*Total market now 13m car passengers   Source: Eurotunnel/Industry estimates

After almost eight years, four cash calls and many bitter battles with TML, the building contractor Eurotunnel will start running a service in six weeks. It is late, over-budget and the competition from ferries will be greater than anticipated at the outset. With the cross-Channel market set to grow rapidly from its present 13m car passengers, Eurotunnel's £7 billion debt is the company's overriding problem.

The cost of the project, originally budgeted at £4.8 billion, is now estimated to be about £10 billion. Because of construction delays, the service, initially expected to come on stream in 1993, will only start in 1994. Its interest bill alone is £600m a year or £11m per week.

Many analysts last week were surprised that the company had pitched its fares so high – ranging from £220 return to £310 – but the company is determined to make Le Shuttle a premium service, arguing that it cannot afford to enter a price war.

Marketing will play a crucial battle for customers. Eurotunnel is investing £25m in a pan-European advertising campaign and the ferry operators are responding with heavyweight publicity for their own services. The ferry operators have invested more than £500m in upgrading short-trip facilities, improving comfort, bringing McDonald's on to ships and turning journeys into entertainment.

Inevitably, however, there will be overcapacity and the ferry operators have already discussed contingency plans, involving the transfer of ships to other routes. 'Unlike Eurotunnel we have got transferable assets,' says a spokesman for Stena. In anticipation of the impact of a powerful new rival, Stena and P&O are hoping that restrictions preventing them from cooperating will be lifted. 'It is the wish of both companies to form joint operations on ticket sales and marketing,' says a Stena spokesman.

(Source: Adapted from *The Sunday Times*, 16 January 1994)

Study the tables and text and answer the following questions.

1 How competitive is the cross-Channel market? Explain your answer. (4)

2 Calculate the average yearly percentage change in the cross-Channel market for the three years 1994–6. (2)

3 a Using Table 1, describe what happened to the revenue forecasts for Eurotunnel. (3)
b Why were the forecasts revised in the way shown in Table 1? (4)
c Why should Eurotunnel be especially worried by revisions of this nature in revenue forecasts? (3)

4 a The cross-Channel market is an oligopolistic market. Explain what this means. (3)
b Using the theory of oligopoly and the information contained in the passage, explain why Eurotunnel argues that 'it cannot afford a price war.' (8)
c In the absence of price competition, in what other ways are the cross-Channel operators competing? (3)
d What other response to Eurotunnel's competition is mentioned in the article? How would this help the cross-Channel operators deal with the new situation? (4)

UK book publishing

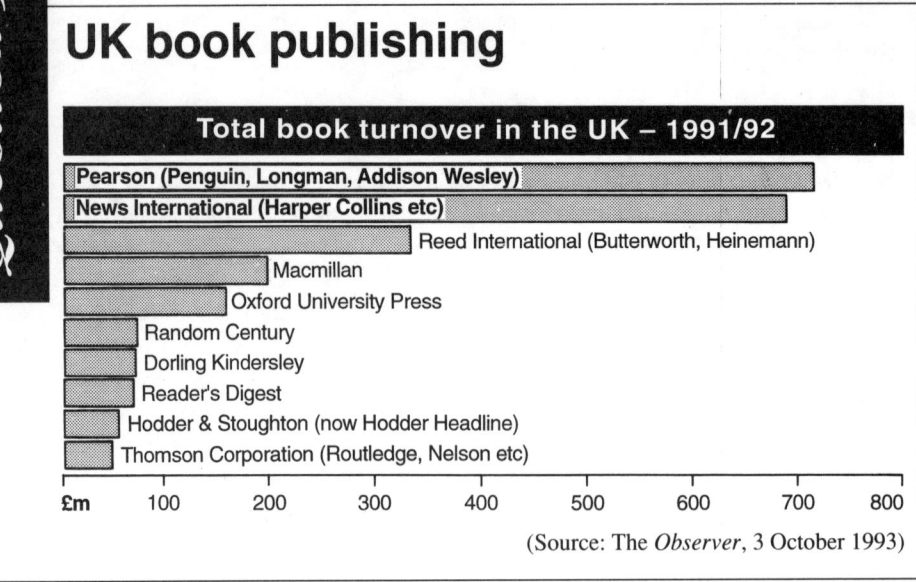

Total book turnover in the UK – 1991/92

Pearson (Penguin, Longman, Addison Wesley)
News International (Harper Collins etc)
Reed International (Butterworth, Heinemann)
Macmillan
Oxford University Press
Random Century
Dorling Kindersley
Reader's Digest
Hodder & Stoughton (now Hodder Headline)
Thomson Corporation (Routledge, Nelson etc)

£m 100 200 300 400 500 600 700 800

(Source: The *Observer*, 3 October 1993)

After studying the figure, answer the following questions.

1 Calculate the concentration ratio for the top three firms in the UK book publishing industry. Show your calculations clearly. (6)

2 Given that the figures relate only to the main publishers, why might the ratio you have calculated not be completely accurate? (2)

3 Using the information provided, what kind of market structure has the book publishing industry? Justify your answer. (3)

4 What are the main factors that cause an industry to have **a** a high and **b** a low concentration ratio? (6)

5 Why might the data underestimate the degree of competition in the UK book publishing industry? (2)

6 Give one other measure on which the concentration ratio for an industry might be based. (1)

CARD SHARP

Mother's Day greetings with massive shop profits attached

More than 34 million Mother's Day cards were sold last week and we shelled out more than £32 million to buy them when they cost only £6 million to make. How do the publishers and retailers get away with it?

On most special occasions consumers only have a limited amount of time to make their choice. And because the purchase is fairly infrequent it makes it difficult to assess what the price really should be.

Cards at Christmas are much cheaper. Two thirds of all cards are sold for that occasion but they account for only one third of the industry's annual swagbag. According to the manufacturers' association, the average buyer wants to send seasonal greetings to more than 50 far-flung friends and relatives, and isn't going to pay a fortune for the privilege. So while you can always buy expensive Christmas cards, the average price is less than 19p.

Some of the smaller greetings card producers work on profit margins of 35%, but all producers find their margins reduced because of wastage. For every 20 designs that are published only 15 will find buyers and even 10% of those that do make it will end up in the pulper. There is a lot of handling involved and that puts a tremendous cost on the product. Publishers use agents to visit hundreds of outlets to keep displays in order and push sales.

The Office of Fair Trading receives regular complaints about card prices, but has concluded that there are no signs of anti-competitive practices distorting the market.

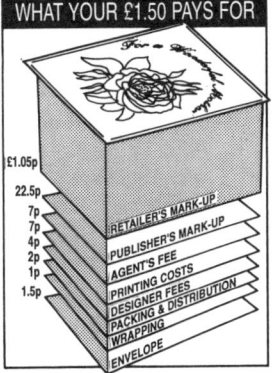

(Source: Adapted from the *Mail on Sunday*, 13 March 1994)

Study the passage and the diagram and answer the following questions.

1 a What are the total production costs of a Mother's Day card? (1)
 b Give examples of (i) a fixed cost and (ii) a variable cost involved in the production of Mother's Day cards. (2)
 c Calculate the retailer's mark-up as a percentage of (i) the price and (ii) the cost of the good. (2)

2 a How would you describe the price elasticity of demand for Mother's Day cards? (2)
 b Explain the factors that have determined the price elasticity of demand for Mother's Day cards. (4)
 c How and why does the price elasticity of demand for Mother's Day cards differ from that of Christmas cards? (5)

3 The Office of Fair Trading has concluded that the high profit mark-up on greetings cards is not a result of anti-competitive behaviour. On what grounds is this conclusion justified? (4)

British rail performance

Table 1 *Passenger transport use and prices*

	Billion passenger kilometres and price indices			
	1981	1986	1989	1990
Use (Great Britain)				
Billion passenger kilometres travelled by:				
Air	3	4	5	5
Rail	34	37	40	40
Road				
Buses and coaches	42	41	41	41
Cars, taxis, and two-wheeled motor vehicles	409	471	563	567
Bicycles	5	5	5	5
Total	493	558	654	658
Retail price indices (United Kingdom) (January 1987 = 100)				
Fares and other travel costs	69	97	115	123
Bus and coach fares	69	98	119	126
Rail fares	69	96	117	128
Motoring expenditure	82	98	114	121
Retail price index (all items)	75	98	115	126

Table 2 *British Rail: passenger business, and investment (Great Britain)*

	1976	1981	1986–87	1990–91
Passenger business				
Passenger carriages (thousands)	17.1	16.2	13.7	12.5
Passenger kilometres per passenger carriage (millions)	1.66	2.10	2.70	3.20
Passenger receipts per passenger kilometre (pence)[1]	5.39	5.76	5.81	6.20
Govt. grants per passenger kilometre (pence)[1]	3.74	4.28	3.04	2.11
Operating expenses per train kilometre (£)[1]	11.7	12.7	10.5	9.3
Investment (£ million)	568	463	509	858

[1]Adjusted for general inflation by the GDP market price deflator (1990–91 prices)

The rail network in Great Britain is made up of the InterCity network, local stopping services, commuter services, and freight and parcel services. The performance of the rail system may be measured by the punctuality of the train services and by the number of train cancellations as well as by the people who use the trains.

One of BR's objectives is to achieve a punctuality standard which requires 90% of trains on InterCity and longer Regional services to arrive within ten minutes of their scheduled time and 92% of trains on the Network SouthEast and 90% on the shorter Regional services to arrive within 5 minutes of their scheduled time. A second objective is a cancellations standard of 1% of current timetabled services for Network SouthEast and shorter Regional and 0.5% for InterCity and longer Regional.

Table 3 *British Rail: performance indicators (Great Britain)*

Percentages

	1986–87[1]	1988–89	1990–91[1]
Percentage of trains arriving within punctuality target			
InterCity sector (10 mins)	85	87	87
Network SouthEast sector			
(5 mins)	91	92	90
Regional sector			
Express and long rural			
(10 mins)	91	90	90
Urban and short rural			
(5 mins)			90
Percentage of trains cancelled			
InterCity sector	0.8	1.0	2.2
Network SouthEast sector	1.6	1.4	2.1
Regional sector			
Express and long rural			1.8
Urban and short rural	0.5	1.2	2.9

[1]Severe winter weather affected some services

(*Source: Adapted from Social Trends 1992.*)

Study the data above, and answer the questions.

1 a Using the information in Table 1, briefly compare the relative importance of railways to total passenger transport for the period 1981–90. (4)
b Using the information in Table 1, calculate what happened to the real price of the three types of travel between 1981 and 1990. (4)
c Does the information obtained in question **1b** help to explain why the relative importance of rail travel to total passenger transport has changed? (2)

2 a What does the economist mean by (i) technical and (ii) allocative efficiency? (4)
b Why might a monopoly like British Rail not achieve either of these efficiency measures? (4)
c What evidence is there in Table 2 that British Rail experienced increased efficiency during the period shown? (2)
d Does Table 2 give any indication as to why efficiency may have increased? (2)
e Explain the meaning of the footnote to Table 2. (2)

3 a Using the data in Table 3 and the objectives set out in the passage, assess British Rail's success in meeting its performance targets. (6)
b What factors, beyond the control of British Rail, may affect its ability to achieve the objectives? (2)

4 The government intends to privatise British Rail in an attempt to improve efficiency. What aspects of privatisation would help or hinder the achievement of this objective? (8)

NICCEA, 1993, paper 3

The macro-economic state of the economy

Shrinking currencies mean growing economies

Whilst the Japanese, German, French and Italian economies are still locked in recession, those of America, Canada, the UK, Australia and New Zealand are all recovering.

The buoyant economies have been helped along by cheap currencies which have enabled them to achieve export-led growth. Broadly speaking, the diagram below shows that the cheaper the currency the faster an economy will grow.

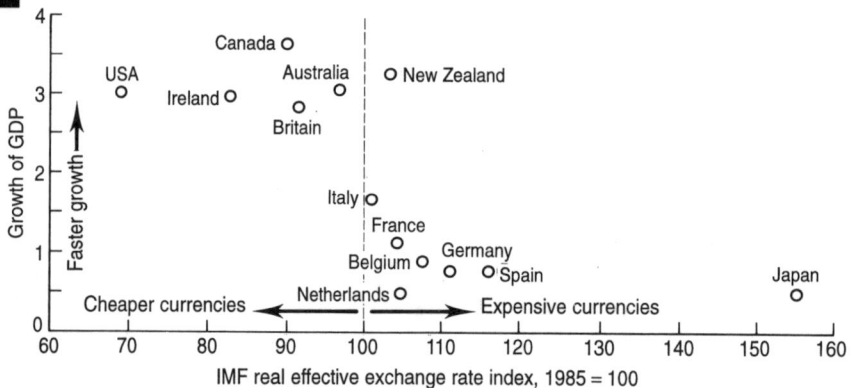

Those Anglo-Saxon countries that are achieving high rates of growth have one thing in common. Their currencies are undervalued because they are exercising a tough fiscal policy with easy money. They have also drawn up workable plans to reduce their budget deficits. On the other hand, Germany, France and Italy have not; and Japan is cutting its taxes and increasing its spending. In continental Europe and in Japan, money is still expensive and scarce.

The mix of fiscal and monetary measures is important. If a country exercises fiscal stringency there will be a deflationary impact on the economy. On the other hand, an expansionary monetary policy is reflationary. It is the impact of these measures on different sectors of the economy that matters. While tax cuts benefit consumers, low interest rates and a cheap currency encourage investment and help companies increase their profits and employment.

For these reasons, countries that have allowed their currencies to shrink have seen their economies grow.

Read the passage and study the diagram. Then answer the following questions.

1 a What is meant by the depreciation of a currency? According to the diagram, which currency has depreciated the most since 1985 and by how much? (3)
   b Does the information on the diagram justify the heading? Explain your answer. (3)

2 a What is meant by the term 'export-led growth'? (2)
   b Why should a cheaper currency encourage exports? Use a numerical example to explain your answer. (4)

c Using the Keynesian diagram of the economy, explain why an increase in exports should cause an economy to grow. (4)

3 a What is meant by the terms (i) 'tough fiscal policy' and (ii) 'easy money', in paragraph 3? (4)
 b Explain the sentence underlined in paragraph 3. (6)

4 Why, in paragraph 4, is it argued that easy money as opposed to less stringent fiscal policy is a better way to stimulate the economy? (4)

Treasury makes big cut in gilts funding needs

Table 1

PSBR by sector (£bn)

	Budget forecast	1993–94 Provisional outturn	1994–95 Forecast
Central government on cash basis			
Receipts:			
Inland Revenue[1]	76.9	77.0	88.5
Customs and Excise[1]	66.9	66.9	73.8
Soc sec contributions (GB)	37.1	36.9	41.7
Interest and dividends	9.1	9.3	8.7
Other	18.4	18.8	19.5
Total receipts	208.4	209.0	232.2
Outlays:			
Interest payments	18.8	18.8	21.7
Privatisation proceeds	−5.4	−5.4	−5.5
Net departmental outlays	245.2	243.4	254.2
Total outlays	258.6	256.9	270.4
Central government borrowing requirement[2]	50.2	47.9	38.1
Local authority borrowing requirement	-0.8	-2.8	-1.0
Public corporations' borrowing requirement	0.4	0.9	-1.0
Public sector borrowing requirement	49.8	46.0	36.1

[1]Payments to the Consolidated Fund
[2]Own account borrowing; excludes net lending to local authorities and public corporations

Outlook fair: the summer forecast

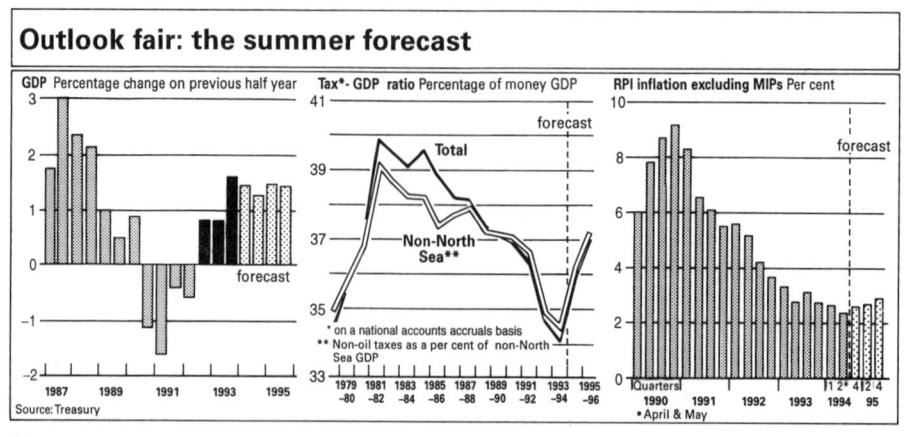

Fig. 1   Fig. 2   Fig. 3

(Source: *The Financial Times*, 29 June 1994)

Study the table and the three figures, and then answer the following questions.

1 What do the initials PSBR stand for? (1)

2 Using the information in Table 1, explain why the PSBR was expected to fall between 1993 and 1995. (4)

3 Describe what was expected to happen to tax revenue over the period covered by Table 1. Does the information in Figures 1, 2 and 3 help explain the expected changes in tax revenue? (8)

4 How is the PSBR funded? (2)

5 Why might the forecast figures for tax revenue and government spending be different from the actual outturn? (4)

6 What problems might the government face in using further fiscal measures to push down the PSBR? (6)

Save more or invest less?

'In the medium term the UK's savings and investment need to come closer into line, and we must ensure that this occurs through a rise in savings rather than a fall in investment.' (John Major)

Table 1
THE FLOW OF FUNDS – 1989 AND 1990

Sectors	Saving				Investment				Balance			
	1989		1990		1989		1990		1989		1990	
	£bn	%of GDP	£bn	%of GDP	£bn	%of GDP	£bn	%of GDP	£bn	%of GDP	£bn	%of GDP
Personal	16.1	3.2	19	3.5	25.6	5.0	25	4.6	−9.5	−1.9	−6	−1.1
Enterprises	39.5	7.8	39	7.2	61.9	12.2	61	11.3	−22.4	−4.4	−22	−4.1
Financial companies	21.2	4.2	21	3.9	14.1	2.8	15	2.8	+7.1	+1.4	+6	+1.1
Governments	14.9	2.9	16	3.0	8.3	1.6	9	1.7	+6.6	+1.3	+7	+1.3
Total domestic	91.7	18.0	95	17.6	109.9	21.6	110	20.4	−18.2	−3.6	−15	−2.8

Sources: *Economic Trends*, April 1990, table A.16.1990: Lloyds Bank forecasts using Treasury assumptions.

Note: Saving includes net capital transfers. Investment includes changes in the book value of stocks. The balance of total domestic sectors should equal the balance of payments. In 1989, because of the residual error of £2.7bn, the balance of payments deficit was £20.9bn. or 4.1 per cent of gdp.

Definition of domestic sectors: personal includes unincorporated businesses; enterprises are industrial and commercial companies and public corporations; financial companies include banks, building societies, insurance companies, and other financial institutions. Governments are central government and local authorities.

(Source: *Lloyds Bank Economic Bulletin*, no. 139, September 1993)

Study the table above and answer the following questions.

1 a What does the economist mean by (i) saving and (ii) investment? (2)
b What are the two categories of investment listed in the expenditure method of the national income accounts? (2)

2 Describe what happened to the pattern of saving in the UK economy between 1989 and 1990. (4)

3 a What is the main component of personal investment? (1)
b What factors could explain the fall in personal and enterprise investment between 1989 and 1990? (4)

4 Explain any fiscal measures that the government could introduce to achieve the equality of saving and investment that John Major wanted. (4)

5 Given the information in the table, what would you expect to happen to interest rates in the economy? Use a diagram to explain your answer. (5)

6 How did the difference between investment and saving change between 1989 and 1990, and how was the difference financed? (3)

It's official: Budget increases will not tax recovery

It's now official. The tax increases of last year's two Budgets will not stall Britain's economic recovery.

The Treasury's summer economic forecast revised up the prediction of UK economic growth this year to 2.75 per cent from 2.5 per cent at the time of last November's Budget.

Although the forecast says growth of consumer spending may slow a little in the short term as a result of tax increases, this is not expected to be reflected in gross domestic product. The Treasury expects the personal savings sector ratio, which fell last year to 11.5 per cent from 12.25 per cent in 1992, will fall further this year to less than 10 per cent. This, and a quickening of disposable income growth to 2.5 per cent next year from 1 per cent in 1994, should enable consumers' expenditure to increase by 3 per cent both this year and next.

Gross domestic product and its components
(£bn at 1990 prices, seasonally adjusted)

	CONSUMERS' EXPENDITURE	GENERAL GOVERNMENT CONSUMPTION	TOTAL FIXED INVESTMENTS	STOCK-BUILDING	DOMESTIC DEMAND	EXPORTS OF GOODS & SERVICES	TOTAL FINAL EXPENDITURE	LESS IMPORTS OF GOODS & SERVICES	LESS ADJUSTMENT TO FACTOR COST	PLUS STATISTICAL DISCREPANCY#	GDP AT FACTOR COST
1993	348.5	116.4	95.3	0.3	560.5	140.3	700.8	153.3	71.8	−0.8	474.9
1994	359.3	118.1	99.2	0.6	577.2	148.9	726.1	162.2	74.5	−1.0	488.4
1995	370.1	118.6	103.2	1.6	593.6	157.2	750.8	170.9	76.9	−1.0	501.9
1993											
1st half	172.5	57.9	47.4	0.4	278.1	69.3	347.4	75.7	35.7	−0.4	235.6
2nd half	176.0	58.5	47.9	0.0	282.4	71.0	353.4	77.6	36.1	−0.5	239.3
1994											
1st half	178.5	58.9	49.4	−0.3	286.5	73.5	360.0	79.9	36.9	−0.5	242.7
2nd half	180.8	59.2	49.8	0.9	290.7	75.4	366.1	82.3	36.7	−0.5	245.7
1995											
1st half	183.6	59.3	51.0	0.7	294.6	77.6	372.2	84.3	38.3	−0.5	249.2
2nd half	186.5	59.3	52.2	0.9	298.9	79.7	378.6	86.6	38.8	−0.5	252.7
PERCENTAGE CHANGES ON A YEAR EARLIER*											
1993	2½	¼	¼	½	2	3	2¼	2¾	2¼	0	2
1994	3	1½	4	0	3	6	3½	5¾	3¾	0	2¾
1995	3	½	4	¼	2¾	5½	3½	5¼	3¼	0	2¾

#Expenditure adjustment *For stockbuilding and the statistical discrepancy, changes are expressed as a percentage of GDP

(Source: Adapted from *The Financial Times*, 29 June 1994)

Read the passage and study the table. Then answer the following questions.

1 What does 'GDP at 1990 prices' mean? (2)

2 a What is the term used for GDP before adjustments for factor cost are made? (1)
 b What adjustments have to be made to convert the figures to factor cost? (2)
 c Why are the factor cost adjustments in the table all negative? (1)
 d What further adjustments would be required to obtain a figure for national income? (4)

3 Explain, using Keynesian analysis, how tax increases could stall economic recovery. (4)

4 Why was it predicted that tax changes would not cause a reduction in consumer spending? (4)

5 Give two other ways in which GDP might be measured. (2)

The UK non-residential property market

Table 1 *The London City Office Market, 1981–1991.*

	Million sq. ft.		
	Available space	Take-up	Market index
1981	1.87	1.99	94
1982	2.68	1.65	162
1983	3.72	2.43	153
1984	3.59	2.48	145
1985	3.00	3.08	97
1986	1.60	3.00	53
1987	1.78	4.17	43
1988	3.35	3.03	111
1989	6.17	3.72	166
1990	9.10	3.11	293
1991	11.30	2.65	426

(Source: City Floorspace Survey, Richard Saunders & Partners)

Market index = balance between supply and demand; if more than 100, supply exceeds demand.

Table 2 *Analysis of the Non-Residential Property Stock in England and Wales, 1991.*

(a) by Capital Value

Per Cent	Retail	Office	Factory	Other	Total
Inner London	4.0	12.8	0.6	4.5	21.9
Outer London	2.3	1.8	1.3	3.4	8.8
Rest of South East	4.7	4.1	3.3	7.9	20.0
Rest of England/Wales	10.5	4.0	8.5	26.3	49.3
Total	**21.5**	**22.7**	**13.7**	**42.1**	**100.0**

(b) by Number

Per Cent	Retail	Office	Factory	Other	Total
Inner London	2.6	2.4	0.9	2.6	8.5
Outer London	3.1	1.1	0.8	2.3	7.3
Rest of South East	5.9	2.8	2.6	7.2	18.5
Rest of England/Wales	21.4	7.5	9.1	27.7	67.7
Total	**33.0**	**13.8**	**13.4**	**39.8**	**100.0**

(Source: Inland Revenue)

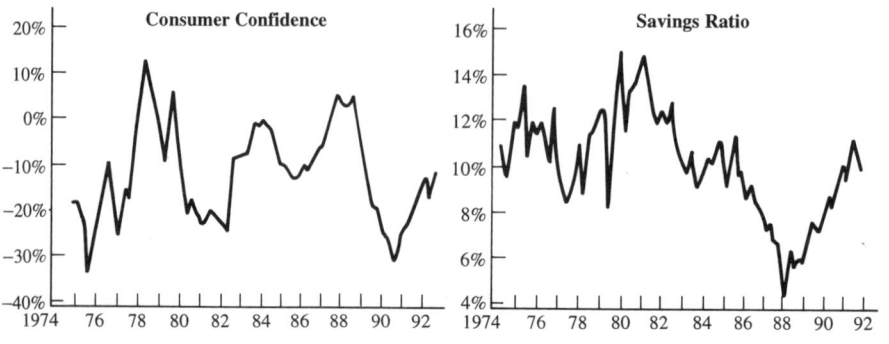

Figure 1

CONSUMER CONFIDENCE

Consumer confidence was measured by means of a survey of consumers conducted by the Gallup organisation. Respondents were asked about their degree of confidence both in the economy as a whole and their personal financial prospects.

The figures in the graph indicate the balance between 'optimists' and 'pessimists'. Zero reflects an even balance, −10% means 55% are pessimists and 45% are optimists, etc.

The lower the figure the greater the weight of pessimism amongst consumers.

SAVINGS RATIO

The proportion of household disposable income which is saved.

(Source: *Barclay's Economic Review*, May 1992)

1 Using the information contained in Table 1, what evidence is there that the non-residential property sector has been affected by the recession? (5)

2 From Table 2, in which part of England and Wales were property values highest in 1991? Explain your answer. (4)

3 Using Table 2, what evidence is there to suggest that the tertiary sector is more important in Inner London than in the rest of England and Wales? (2)

4 a Use Figure 1 to explain what happened to consumer confidence and the savings ratio between 1988 and 1992. (3)
b How might you account for the relationship between consumer confidence and the savings ratio? (3)

5 a What factors would influence the savings ratio? (4)
b Is it important to distinguish between the average propensity to save and the marginal propensity to save? (4)

6 a Why is consumer confidence regarded as an important economic indicator? (3)
b What factors might influence consumer confidence? (3)
c What problems may arise in measuring consumer confidence? (4)

NICCEA, 1993, paper 3

Components of UK GDP using the expenditure method

Annual % real change

	1989/90	1990/91	1991/92	1992/93	1993/94	1994/95
Real output growth	2.1	0.6	−2.5	−0.5	2.0	2.6
Consumer spending	3.3	0.7	−2.0	0.0	2.0	2.2
Gross fixed investment	7.2	−3.1	−9.9	−0.5	2.5	5.0
General govt spending	0.9	3.2	3.2	0.0	−1.1	
Exports	3.5	4.9	0.1	2.7	5.6	
Imports	7.4	1.0	−3.1	5.6	4.9	

(Source: CSO and London Business School of Econometric Model)

Study the table and answer the following questions.

1 Describe the state of the British economy during the years 1989 to 1994. (8)

2 a Explain briefly the accelerator theory of investment. (4)
 b Does the data provide any evidence for the accelerator theory of investment? (3)

3 Why should government spending have increased so much in 1990/91? (3)

4 a What happened to the balance of payments over the period covered by the data? (3)
 b Is the demand for imports into the UK income elastic or inelastic? (Show your calculations.) (4)

Ulster acquires prosperity without economic strength

Not only has the province weathered the 1990s' economic recession better than any other region of the UK, but those elusive green shoots of recovery are also appearing there in more profusion than anywhere on the mainland.

The latest bunch of economic data and forecasts indicate that not only is unemployment falling steadily in Northern Ireland, but according to the London economic consultancy Business Strategies, 'in 1993 every sector of the province's economy is set to outperform the UK'.

Any attempt to extrapolate this cheery outlook to the mainland economy must, however, take account of two crucial factors that have helped cushion the severity of this recession in Northern Ireland. According to the Northern Ireland Economic Research Centre, 'unlike the recession in the early 1980s, which was driven by a high exchange rate, this recession has been driven by high interest rates and mortgage debt.'

The second factor has been the role played by public sector spending in the province. Forty per cent of the workforce in Northern Ireland is employed in the public sector, including the security forces, compared with 20 per cent nationally. This is reflected in the fact that Northern Ireland is a net receiver of Exchequer funds to the tune of £3.5 billion, and is perhaps a warning to anyone wishing to draw a lesson from Northern Ireland's economic performance.

Mr Michael Smyth of the Department of Applied Economics at the University of Ulster says: 'Northern Ireland has the highest regional population of two-income families, partly due to the large public sector here. So the drop in consumer demand during the recession has been nothing like as severe as on the mainland. Bank lending has continued to grow throughout the recession. The latest figures on hire purchase credit also show that we have definitely turned the corner.'

However, he was cautious on the long term prospects. 'The economy here is demand driven by public spending and by demand from the mainland. Any real growth will be determined by the recovery in Great Britain.'

'Weaker competitiveness will also act as a brake. Competitiveness here is poor compared to Great Britain and that basic weakness is likely to remain into the foreseeable future.' Lower levels of management skills and higher levels of long term unemployment, also due to a shortage of shop-floor skills, are widely considered to be behind lower productivity in the province.

The promising signals of recovery in Northern Ireland tell only part of the story. Anyone wishing to draw comfort from them can have little cause for complacency.

(Source: Adapted from *The Financial Times*, 18 May 1993)

Read the whole passage carefully before answering the questions.

1 a In the first paragraph, the article refers to 'elusive green shoots . . . appearing in profusion'. What is meant by this? (2)
b List three 'green shoots'. (3)

2 a Explain the statement 'this recession has been driven by high interest rates and mortgage debt' (paragraph 3). (3)
b Why should this have resulted in Northern Ireland being cushioned from the severity of the recession in the early 1990s? (2)
c How might high exchange rates have caused the previous recession mentioned in paragraph 3? (3)

3 What other factors cushioned Northern Ireland from the effects of the recession? (3)

4 a What is meant by competitiveness? (2)
b Why is competitiveness in Northern Ireland lower than in the rest of the United Kingdom? (4)

5 If competitiveness is the problem in the Northern Ireland economy, list three supply-side measures which might be used to deal with this. (3)

Unemployment

Britain's labour market turns dramatically

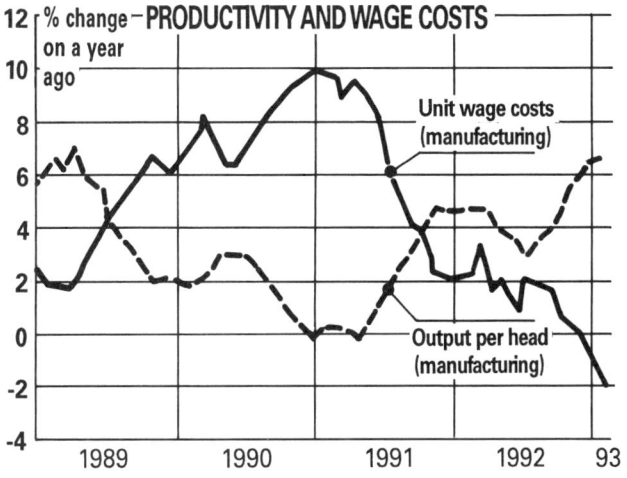

Fig. 1

Fig. 2

(Source: *The Sunday Times*, 25 April 1993)

Study the two diagrams and answer the following questions.

1 In what year or years did output per head actually fall? (1)

2 a What is the relationship between unit wage costs and output per head? (2)
b What factors could explain the changes in output per head? (3)
c Does the fall in unit wage costs in 1991 imply that wages fell during that year? (2)

3 a What is meant by a three-month moving average? Explain how it is obtained. (3)
b What is the difference between the three-month moving average unemployment figures and the actual figures? Why should this be the case? (3)
c What is the term used to describe the alteration of the actual unemployment figures by the use of moving averages? (1)

4 a Name four different types of unemployment. (4)
b What types of unemployment are illustrated in Figure 2? Explain your answer. (4)
c In which months did the level of unemployment fall? (2)

Regional unemployment in the UK

Regional unemployment rates in the UK, 1990–93 (%)

	1990	1991	1992	1993
England				
North	8.6	10.6	11.2	11.2
Yorkshire & Humberside	6.8	9.1	9.9	9.8
East Midlands	5.1	7.8	8.7	9
East Anglia	3.8	6.2	7.1	8.3
South-East	3.9	7.4	9.4	10.3
South-West	4.5	7.7	9.1	9.2
West Midlands	5.9	9	10.7	11.6
North-West	7.5	9.9	10.1	10.9
Wales	6.6	9.2	8.9	9.5
Scotland	8	9.2	9.5	10.1
Northern Ireland	13.7	14.1	12.1	12.5
UNITED KINGDOM	**6.8**	**8.7**	**9.9**	**9.6**

(Source: *Regional Trends*, 1994)

Study the data in the table and answer the following questions.

1 a What happened to the geographical distribution of unemployment in the UK between 1990 and 1993? (4)
b Which area experienced the most rapid increase in unemployment during the period covered by the data? (1)

2 Account for the changing geographical distribution of unemployment during the years covered by the data. (6)

3 Apart from the data about the geographical distribution of unemployment, what other unemployment statistics would the government require as an aid to economic policy? (4)

4 In the past the government has actively tried to change the geographical distribution of unemployment.
a Why would it wish to do this? (3)
b What policies might be used to achieve this goal? (3)
c What are the economic arguments against government intervention of this nature? (4)

Inflation

Cash rich

But where is it all coming from?

Are you carrying a lot of cash around? If so 'Steady' Eddie George, the Governor of the Bank of England, would like to know why.

Unbelievable though it may seem to those of us who all too often find our wallets empty, there has been a near 10 per cent growth so far this year in the MO money supply. The worry of course is that this means inflation is taking off again due to the economy 'overheating'. Eddie has been particularly angry to see prices of building materials shoot up and has accused industry of under-investing. But in fact output prices, the measure of inflation at the factory gate, was only 1.9 per cent in June – the lowest since 1967.

It is my guess that the jump in MO is due to factors like the 'black economy' – for example car boot sales, which have grown fast, and second-hand car sales. Also it could be that because you get less interest from leaving money in a building society or bank, many people are now carrying a bigger wad.

Whatever the reason, the uncertainty led to a 'flop' in the last auction by the Bank of England of £2 billion of government stock. This was only a 'flop' in the sense that it was only 1.3 times oversubscribed instead of the expected 1.7 times.

These government stocks are at what I regard as bargain levels on a long-term view. A suitable government stock for a small investor to buy is the Treasury nine per cent 2012 at £104. Buy £100 nominal of this stock and you are guaranteed £9 a year interest for 18 years ahead. No, I do not expect you to hold it that long. But I do expect you to be able to clear a good capital profit one day when interest rates do come down. They surely cannot remain at seven per cent over the inflation rate – twice the norm. Another optimistic sign is that the PSBR is likely to be nearer £30bn than the expected £50bn.

Remember you read the good news here first!

(Source: *Belfast News Letter*, 9 August 1994)

Read the passage and answer the questions below.

1 a What is the MO money supply? (1)
  b Why should an expansion of the 'black economy' cause an increase in MO? (2)
  c What is the broader M4 definition of the money supply comprised of? (2)
  d Why should economists be concerned about the effect of a rising money supply on the rate of inflation? (4)

2 a What is meant by the economy 'overheating'? (2)
  b Give three indicators that would show the economy is overheating. (3)
  c Explain how 'under-investing' by industry could result in the economy overheating. (4)

3 a Why does the Bank of England sell government stock? (1)
  b What does 'Treasury nine per cent 2012 at £104' stock mean? (2)
  c Explain why a fall in interest rates should enable investors in government stock to make a capital gain. (4)

4 a What was the real interest rate earned by investors in August 1994? (1)
  b Why was it expected that interest rates would fall? (4)

300 years of inflation

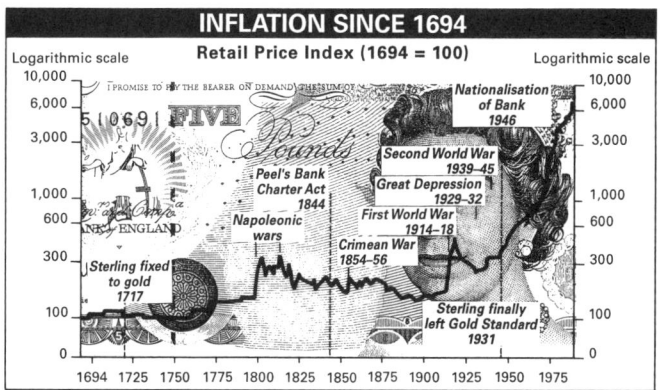

INFLATION SINCE 1694

Retail Price Index (1694 = 100)

Logarithmic scale

Nationalisation of Bank 1946

Second World War 1939–45

Peel's Bank Charter Act 1844

Great Depression 1929–32

Napoleonic wars

First World War 1914–18

Crimean War 1854–56

Sterling fixed to gold 1717

Sterling finally left Gold Standard 1931

1694 1725 1750 1775 1800 1825 1850 1875 1900 1925 1950 1975

The Bank of England was founded in 1694 by King William III. If at the same time he had established the retail price index with a value of 100, then today the index would stand at approximately 6700, a rise of 6600 per cent. This is not a particularly surprising figure as we have come to accept inflation as part of the natural order of life. However, what should surprise us is that almost all of this rise has occurred in the last 50 years.   5

The pound held its value all through the reigns of Queen Victoria, Queen Anne, George I and George II. It took 254 years and three great European wars for prices to treble. Since then, in a time of peace, they have multiplied by 20.

Where did we go wrong this time? The chart shows that inflation soared from the moment that the Bank was nationalised in 1946. Since then the Bank has been little more than an arm   10 of government in an era when state activities have expanded continuously. This gave the Bank and the government a vested interest in inflation. They soon found that printing more money was the simplest way to pay their bills. They also found that it made their debt less burdensome to them and worth less to those who had invested in gilts.

Post-war governments were able to persuade themselves that inflation was good for us as   15 well as being good for them. They took the convenient view that there was a trade-off between price stability and full employment. If employment started to fall and the economy faltered, they need only press down on the inflationary accelerator and all would be well.

Not for long though. This nice relationship went sadly astray and governments found themselves facing both rising inflation and rising unemployment. It was time for a rethink,   20 and this was provided by Mrs Thatcher who succeeded in reducing both the rate of inflation and the state's share of GDP.

Alas! Inflation is not yet dead and buried. There is a depressingly familiar look about the current state of government finances.

Any government that absorbs, as ours does, getting on for half the national income, and   25 spends much of it unproductively, will always be tempted to pay its way with printed promises. A government that increases the size of its debt by one third in one year, as ours did last year, will always be tempted to let inflation make that debt less burdensome.

Inflation is the result of big government and its elimination will require a reappraisal of the range of activities which we expect governments to perform.   30

(Source: Adapted from the *Daily Telegraph*, 9 May 1994)

Read the passage and answer the following questions.

1 If the Bank of England had issued a pound note in 1694, what would its real value be in 1994? (2)

2 Explain the relationship between government spending and inflation referred to in paragraph 3. (4)

3 Explain why holders of gilts lose because of inflation and why governments gain (lines 13–14). (6)

4 In lines 16–17 the author refers to 'a trade-off between price stability and full employment'. By what name is this relationship commonly known? (2)

5 Describe what happened to this relationship in the 1960s and 1970s. (4)

6 Do you agree with the author's conclusion that only a substantial reduction in government expenditure can deliver the elimination of inflation? Explain your answer. (7)

Treasury to veto Bank's independence

The government has checked the Bank of England's hopes of gaining full independence. Senior Treasury sources have made clear that, while the Bank has been given a greater say in monetary policy decisions, it will not get Bundesbank-style autonomy.

Asked why the Bank would not be given complete freedom to set interest rates, the source said: 'Because nobody has ever voted for Eddie George'. This will dash the hopes of George, the Bank of England governor, who has campaigned hard for independence. He has made it clear publicly and privately that he sees an independent and accountable central bank as best able 'to deliver low inflation, more stable growth, better economic performance and lower interest rates'.

The government's views are confirmed by the Treasury's response to the all-party House of Commons Treasury and Civil Service committee. The response says: 'The government believes that present institutional arrangements, including the new provision for publishing the minutes of the chancellor's monthly meetings with the governor, are fully capable of meeting the targets the government has set for inflation.'

Kenneth Clarke, the chancellor, said last week that there was no difference between him and the governor on the aims of policy. 'I share the aim of low inflation and sound money,' he said. 'Steady Eddie meets canny Ken, you could say.'

However, some in the Treasury are angered by the Bank's conduct since the last cut in base rates in early February, when rates were trimmed from 5.5% to 5.25%. News of the Bank's opposition to the cut soon leaked out to the financial markets, undermining sentiment. And, following the release of minutes that confirmed the Bank had opposed the move, it dwelt on the damage that the rate-cut had done in its May inflation report.

One interesting question will be whether George keeps up his public campaign for independence. He warned earlier this year that those who argued that interest-rate decisions should be left in the hands of politicians were saying, in effect, 'that governments should retain the option of debasing the currency'.

Since the Bank has been given a greater say in monetary policy decisions, the City has been paying far more attention to its utterances on the economy. The Bank has, however, blotted its copybook by regularly overpredicting inflation. In its quarterly report released on May 10, it predicted that April's underlying inflation rate would show a rise to 2.8% from 2.4%. In the event, official figures published eight days later showed a fall to 2.3%.

(Source: Adapted from *The Sunday Times*, 22 May 1994)

Read the passage and answer the following questions.

1 What does it mean to give the Bank of England full independence? (2)

2 Why should an independent central bank be better able 'to deliver low inflation, more stable growth, better economic performance and lower interest rates'? (5)

3 What is the case against an independent central bank? (5)

4 a Monetarists believe that inflationary expectations are as important as government economic policy in combating inflation. Explain why this is the case. (3)
b How would the difference of opinion between the Bank of England and the chancellor over the cutting of the base rate from 5.5 per cent to 5.25 per cent damage the government in the battle against inflation? (3)

5 Why should governments wish to debase the currency as Eddie George suggests in paragraph 6? (4)

6 The Bank of England forecast for inflation in April 1994 was nearly 25 per cent too high. Why do economists often get forecasts wrong? (3)

International trade and exchange rates

Industry raises warning over future growth

Strong pound threatens exporters

Industry is increasingly worried about the impact on recovery of April's tax rises and the pound's rise against the D-mark, the Confederation of British Industry (CBI) will say tomorrow.

The CBI has favoured an export-led recovery but its members fear the pound's recovery against European currencies is hitting export opportunities. Many see a DM2.60 sterling rate as a watershed, and warn that a big rise in the pound above that – which currency analysts expect – will be a serious blow for exporters. Sterling closed at DM2.61 on Friday.

There are also growing fears that tax increases will hit the consumer in Britain hard, while other markets are still struggling to recover. Many CBI members favour a pre-emptive strike by the chancellor on base rates, both to hold down the pound and to head off the damaging impact of the tax rises. Without such action, the concern is that industry will face a double blow, with both home and export markets hit.

Firms are also cautious about the employment outlook. In spite of recent official figures showing falling unemployment, most manufacturers expect to cut staff. This month has seen announcements of large-scale redundancies from British Aerospace, as well as the high-street banks. Although the January CBI survey normally shows a significant boost in price increases by manufacturers, the latest survey is set to show that most firms still see competitive pressures as restraining prices.

The Treasury has taken comfort from the fact that, in spite of last week's announcement of a 0.2% fall in retail sales in December, consumer confidence is slowly recovering. The EC-Gallup survey of consumer confidence, published this weekend, shows an improvement from minus 18 to minus 12 when pessimists are measured against optimists. Ministers and officials believe this shows consumer spending can withstand the impact of the April tax increases.

(Source: Adapted from *The Sunday Times*, 21 January 1994)

Read the passage from *The Sunday Times* and answer the following questions.

1 What economic indicators are used in this article to justify the worries of the CBI about Britain's economic recovery? (5)

2 a What is meant by the phrase 'export-led recovery' in paragraph 2? (2)
b Using a numerical example, explain how the rise in the price of the pound against the Deutschmark will be 'a serious blow for exporters'. (5)
c What is the CBI assuming about the price elasticity of demand for British exports? Explain the connection between the rising exchange rate, export-led growth and the price elasticity of demand for exports. (5)

3 a Explain what is meant by the 'base rate' in paragraph 3. (1)

 b What does the CBI want the chancellor to do with the base rate? (1)

 c How would a change in the base rate (i) 'hold down the pound' and (ii) 'head off the damaging impact of tax rises'? (6)

4 a What is consumer confidence (paragraph 5)? (2)

 b What does it mean that consumer confidence has improved from minus 18 to minus 12? (3)

 c Why should an improvement in confidence give comfort to the Treasury? (2)

Direct investment into the UK

International trade has always been important to the UK, a relatively open economy. But in recent years, international direct investment flows have also grown in significance. The tables below give some information about direct investment into the UK during the 1980s.

(Source: *Lloyds Bank Economic Bulletin*, no. 138, June 1990)

Table 1
FOREIGN DIRECT INVESTMENT INFLOWS
Top 10 countries ranked by size of inflow, 1988

Country	Inflow $bn 1988	Inflow % of gnp	Annual nominal growth % 1983–88
USA	58.5	1.2	37
UK	13.9	1.9	22
France	8.5	1.0	37
Spain	7.0	2.3	34
Italy	6.8	0.9	42
Australia	5.4	2.6	13
Benelux	5.1	3.4	32
Canada	3.9	0.9	18
Netherlands	3.6	1.7	21
W Germany	1.6	0.2	4

(Source: *IMF Balance of Payments Statistics & World Bank Atlas.*)

Table 2
FOREIGN-OWNED MANUFACTURING PRODUCTION IN THE UK
Top 8 countries ranked by gross UK output, 1987

	Gross output £m	Employ-ment '000s	Net output per head £000s	Inputs of raw materials and semi-finished goods % of output	Capital spending per head £000s
USA	33112	384	34	61	3.1
Canada	3581	48	31	59	3.4
Switzerland	2147	32	24	65	3.4
France	1940	23	46	47	2.4
Netherlands	1714	30	27	54	2.7
Germany	1630	23	31	56	3.1
Australia	1308	13	53	48	2.5
Japan	1083	11	22	79	8.3
Totals:					
foreign-controlled	50936	625	32	60	3.2
domestic-controlled	191905	4048	21	55	1.8

(Source: *1987 Census of Production, Business Monitor PA 1002*)

Study the tables and answer the following questions.

1 a What is meant by a 'foreign direct investment inflow'? (2)
b Where would a foreign direct investment inflow show on the balance of payments accounts? (1)
c In the long run, what effects would a foreign direct investment inflow have on the balance of payments accounts? (3)
d How would foreign investment in the UK, which was financed locally, be treated in the balance of payments accounts? Explain your answer. (3)

2 a What is meant by 'annual nominal growth' in Table 1? (1)
b From the data in Table 1, assess how well the UK performed in attracting inward investment. (4)

3 a What would explain the difference between productivity in foreign-controlled firms and productivity in domestically controlled firms in Table 2? (3)
b How has the figure for net output per head in Table 2 been calculated? (2)

4 Explain the factors which would account for the attraction of the UK as a destination for foreign direct investment. (6)

British merchant shipping

Table 1 *The UK Owned Trading Fleet, 500 gross registered tons (grt) and above. Selected Years, 1975–1991*

(End Year)	1975		1985		1987		1989		March 1991	
Register	mdwt	no	mdwt	no	mdwt	no	mdwt	no	mdwt	no
Mainland UK	50	1614	15.3	586	6.0	386	4.9	336	3.8	312
Crown Dependencies[a]	negligible		0.2	24	3.5	77	2.7	71	2.7	67
Dependent Territories[b]	N/A[c]		2.7	82	6.3	99	5.6	81	4.9	78
Foreign	N/A[c]		1.8	90	1.8	93	2.0	93	3.8	127
Total Fleet	50	1614	20.0	782	17.6	655	15.2	581	15.2	584

Notes: (a) Crown Dependencies: Isle of Man and Channel Islands
(b) British Dependent Territories: these include Bermuda, Cayman Islands, Gibraltar and Hong Kong
(c) Not available
Source: General Council of British Shipping

Table 2 *Bulk Carrier Vessels, Differences in Manning Costs*

Flag	Officers	Ratings	Cost (US$pa)
UK	UK	UK	955,000
Hong Kong	UK/Indian	Filipino	446,000
Liberian/Filipino	Filipino	Filipino	367,000

Source: P & O 1987

Table 3 *Sea Transport, Balance of Payments Account 1979–1989 (£ million)*

	1979	1981	1983	1985	1987	1989
Ships owned or chartered in by UK residents	1212	1116	410	707	897	1139
Ships operated by overseas residents	−1030	−1203	−1032	−1004	−932	−1109
Overall balance – Sea Transport	182	−87	−622	−297	−35	30

(Source: The *Royal Bank of Scotland Review*, no. 171, September 1991)

Study the tables and answer the questions below.

1 a What trends are illustrated in the figures on UK-owned shipping given in Table 1? (6)
b Using the information in Tables 1 and 3, calculate the average export earnings per UK registered ship in 1989. (2)

2 a Using the figures in Table 2, calculate the percentage reduction in manning costs as a result of using foreign crews in place of all-British crews. (2)
b What factors, other than wages, might help explain the changes in the size of the UK fleet between 1975 and 1991? (6)

3 a Using the data in Table 3, trace the impact of sea transport on the UK balance of payments. (4)
b In what section of the balance of payments accounts would 'sea transport' be found? (1)

4 Apart from the effects on the balance of payments, what are the other economic implications of the changes in the UK merchant shipping industry? (4)

Improving Britain's competitiveness

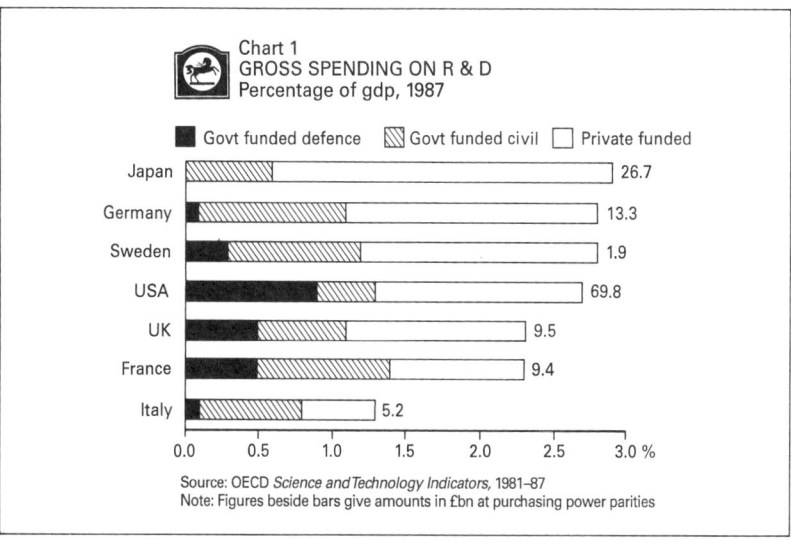

Chart 1
GROSS SPENDING ON R & D
Percentage of gdp, 1987

■ Govt funded defence   ▨ Govt funded civil   □ Private funded

Japan	26.7
Germany	13.3
Sweden	1.9
USA	69.8
UK	9.5
France	9.4
Italy	5.2

0.0   0.5   1.0   1.5   2.0   2.5   3.0 %

Source: OECD *Science and Technology Indicators*, 1981–87
Note: Figures beside bars give amounts in £bn at purchasing power parities

(Source: *Lloyds Bank Economic Bulletin*, no. 134, February 1990)

Study the chart and answer the following questions.

1 Using the data in the chart, compare spending on research and development (R & D) in the UK with that of the other OECD countries. (5)

2 a The figures are converted to £ billions using purchasing power parities (PPP). What does this mean? (4)
b Why is the PPP method of conversion sometimes used rather than converting at the exchange rate established on the foreign exchange market? (3)

3 a R & D spending is regarded as a supply-side measure. What does this mean? (2)
b Using an appropriate diagram, show how supply-side measures could promote economic growth. (3)

4 R & D spending helps an economy to remain competitive. What other factors help to maintain and improve competitiveness? (4)

5 The report from which this chart was taken concludes, 'UK official R & D spending needs to be diverted away from defence and be increased on civilian products and services.' Why is R & D spending on defence regarded as less desirable than R & D spending on civilian products? (3)

The cost of Black Wednesday

On Wednesday 16th September 1992, after weeks of speculation, the government finally had to admit defeat and the pound left the ERM which Mrs Thatcher had reluctantly joined in 1989.

The political cost of the ERM fiasco eventually resulted in the fall of Norman Lamont, the Chancellor of the Exchequer, and a loss of credibility for the government. The amount of money spent by the Bank of England in <u>the government's failed attempt to prop up the pound</u> has been estimated at anything between £10bn and £20bn. This was used to buy up pounds in order to keep the value of the pound above <u>the ERM floor</u>.

The final cost of the exercise was determined by the rate which prevailed when the Bank of England 'closed out' its intervention, by converting the pounds which it bought during the week before 16th September 1992 back into other currencies.

By Friday 18th September the pound had fallen to DM2.60. If £15bn had been spent in an effort to support sterling and it was all converted at this rate, which was 6.5% below DM2.77 – the price at which most intervention took place – then the loss would have been £975m. Depending on the rate at which the £15bn was converted, this loss could be greater or smaller.

The real effects of the loss of £975bn can be measured in many ways. It amounts to 20% of the road building programme in the UK and, if it had been available to the health service, the building of new hospitals could have been increased by 60%. Had the money been available for overseas aid, it could have supplied all the aid needs in Somalia for a full year.

As it is, <u>the direct beneficiaries of Britain's attempt to stay in the ERM by propping up the pound are the speculators</u>.

1 What is meant by the three phrases underlined in the passage? (9)

2 What was the opportunity cost of the Bank of England's attempt to intervene on behalf of the pound? (2)

3 a Explain, with the aid of a diagram, how the Bank of England's intervention was supposed to prevent the pound falling through the ERM floor. (3)
b What other actions might have been taken and how would they have helped to prop up the value of the pound? (3)

4 What factors could have caused sterling's slide? (3)

5 a Explain why the cost of propping up the pound was not £10–£20 billion, even though that was the amount spent on intervention by the Bank. (2)
b Assuming the Bank used DM28 billion to buy pounds when sterling was worth DM2.80, and subsequently 'closed out' its intervention when sterling had fallen to DM2.50, how much was lost in sterling? (3)

Non-EU trade gap falls sharply

Fig. 1 | Non-EU trade: balance and volume |

(a)
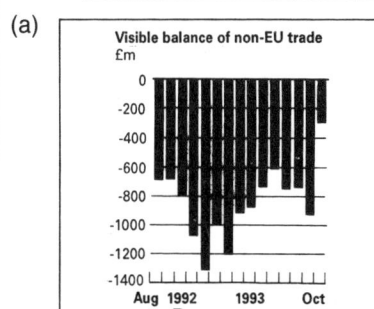
Visible balance of non-EU trade
£m
Source: CSO

(b)
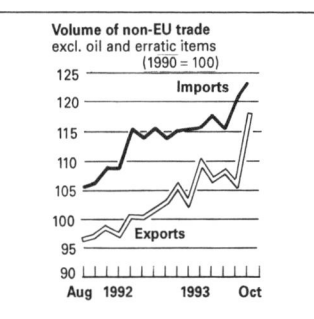
Volume of non-EU trade
excl. oil and erratic items
(1990 = 100)

Table 1 Non-EU trade: value

Balance-of-payments basis, seasonally adjusted (£m)

		Exports	Imports	Balance	Excl oil and erratics* Exports	Imports	Balance
1991		44 477	53 883	−9 406	38 289	45 250	−6 961
1992		46 682	56 431	−9 749	40 624	48 097	−7 473
1992	Q2	11 665	13 856	−2 191	10 128	11 776	−1 648
	Q3	11 577	13 675	−2 098	10 069	11 667	−1 598
	Q4	12 134	15 295	−3 161	10 574	13 119	−2 545
1993	Q1	13 670	16 765	−3 095	11 762	14 066	−2 304
	Q2	14 205	16 421	−2 216	12 026	14 131	−2 105
	Q3	14 602	16 995	−2 393	12 606	14 484	−1 878
May		4 665	5 408	−743	3 922	4 746	−824
June		4 863	5 468	−605	4 133	4 660	−527
July		4 847	5 591	−744	4 173	4 848	−675
August		4 905	5 633	−728	4 204	4 744	−540
September		4 850	5 771	−921	4 229	4 892	−663
October		5 276	5 569	−293	4 686	5 016	−330

Defined as ships, aircraft, precious stones and silver

Britain's trade deficit with countries outside the European Union fell sharply to its lowest level for nearly six years last month as exports jumped to records in value terms.

The October deficit, the smallest with non-EU countries since January 1988 – when the CSO first published such figures – reflected a jump of nearly 9 per cent in the value of exports to £5.28bn last month. At the same time imports fell 3.5 per cent to £5.57bn. Exports of finished manufactures, food and fuels rose sharply last month in volume terms.

Yesterday's figures suggest that UK exporters are taking advantage of stronger growth in the US. The £138m surplus in north American trade in October was the highest since March 1989.

Taking the three-month figures, which the government says give a better guide to trends, exports in August, September and October were 4.5 per cent higher in value terms than in the May–July period, while imports rose 3 per cent. Compared with the same period last year, exports were 28 per cent higher and imports 22 per cent higher.

In volume terms, exports were 2 per cent higher in the latest three months compared with the three months to the end of July, while imports were up 4 per cent. Volume exports and imports were up 14 per cent and 12 per cent respectively compared with August–October 1992.

(Source: Adapted from *The Financial Times*, 20 November 1993)

Read the passage and study the diagrams and table before answering the following questions.

1 What is meant by the term 'visible balance of non-EU trade' in Figure 1(a)? (2)

2 a Using the information in Figure 1, describe what happened to the visible balance of non-EU trade between October 1992 and September 1993. (4)
b Using the information in Table 1, measure the size of the trade deficit with the non EU-countries for the 12 months October 1992 to September 1993. (3)

3 a How does the balance calculated in question **2b** compare with the balance which excludes erratic items? (2)
b Why are erratic items and oil excluded from the figures? Why should ships, aircraft, precious stones and silver be defined as erratic items? (4)

4 Using Figure 1(b) and paragraphs 4 and 5, explain why the changes in the UK balance of trade recorded between October 1992 and September 1993 occurred. (3)

5 a Explain the phrase 'UK exporters are taking advantage of stronger growth in the US' (paragraph 3). (2)
b How can strong US growth improve the UK balance of payments? (3)

6 Explain what is meant, in the last paragraph, by an increase in exports in volume terms. (2)

Spares lead the way in India car parts exports

Component makers take advantage of trade liberalisation reforms

Lumax industries, a Delhi-based company, is one of India's most recent entrants to export markets, selling spare-part lights for Volkswagen, Mercedes and Rover cars and for Italian-made Iveco lorries. 'They're half the price of the original manufacturers' equipment,' says Mr A K Sethi, the export manager. 'Our labour is cheap but we have to watch other costs.'

India's main advantages in the market are low-cost labour, lax environmental controls for 'dirty' industries, and a long engineering tradition. Indian industry executives say India is a cost-effective country for hot and dirty operations, among them casting and forging of heavy components such as axles and transmission drives. It could also be a competitive supplier of electrical components, particularly those that might require manual assembly.

However, Indian suppliers suffer from serious disadvantages, including inadequate infrastructure and a reputation for poor quality, which blights Indian exports generally. For these reasons large western and Japanese groups have often shied away from buying Indian components. Indian manufacturers have relied instead on the spares market, where buyers have been more easily swayed by low prices.

But there are signs that Indian companies' prospects are improving rapidly. The slow-down in car demand in industrialised countries has forced big groups to cut costs further than before, so the pressure to find reliable low-cost sources has increased. At the same time, Indian executives are steadily learning what they must do to meet foreign buyers' expectations.

One US car company executive visiting Delhi said India as a whole had no particular advantage over other countries as a parts supplier. Low-cost labour was no use if it meant low productivity and poor quality, he said. What mattered more was how a company made use of low-cost labour.

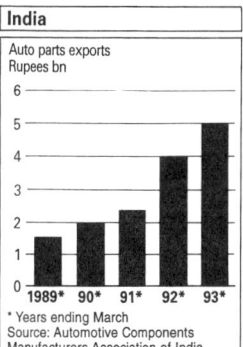

India

Auto parts exports
Rupees bn

* Years ending March
Source: Automotive Components
Manufacturers Association of India

(Source: Adapted from *The Financial Times*, 28 January 1994)

Read the passage and study the table. Then answer the following questions.

1 Using 1990 as the base year, construct an index to show what happened to Indian exports of auto parts during the period 1989–93. (8)

2 a Explain what is meant by comparative advantage. (4)
b In what kind of production does India have the comparative advantage over western countries and Japan? Why has India achieved the comparative advantage in these types of production? (5)

3 a What are the two main markets for auto parts? (2)
b Explain what economists mean by price elasticity of demand. (2)
c In which of the markets for auto parts is demand most price elastic, and why do you think this is the case? (5)

4 How might world economic conditions help the Indian auto parts industry? (2)

5 What is meant by the statement made by the US company executive at the end of the article? (3)

Tax and government spending

Who gets the Peace Dividend?

The phrase 'peace dividend' has been coined in the USA to express the hope that the new era of disarmament and detente will result in major savings in defence expenditure. The table and diagrams below illustrate the size and impact of defence spending on various economies.

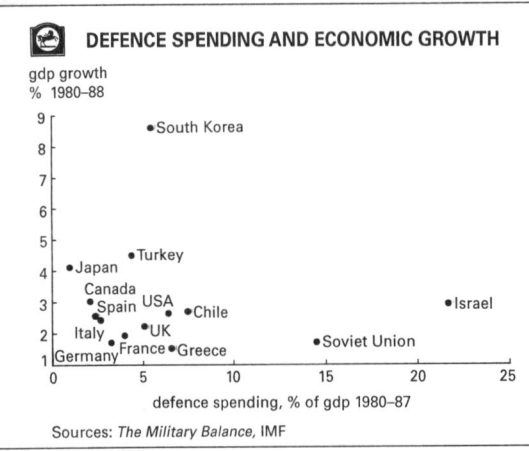

DEFENCE SPENDING AND ECONOMIC GROWTH

gdp growth
% 1980–88

Sources: *The Military Balance, IMF*

Fig. 1

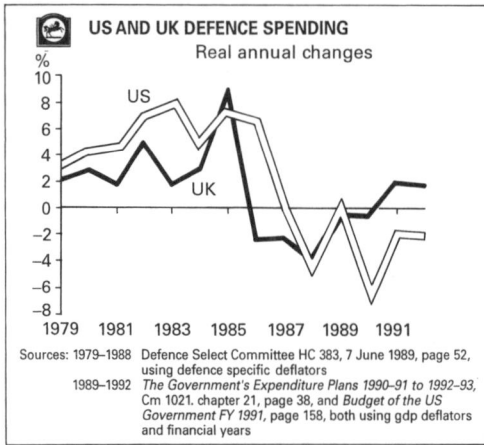

US AND UK DEFENCE SPENDING
Real annual changes

Sources: 1979–1988 Defence Select Committee HC 383, 7 June 1989, page 52, using defence specific deflators
1989–1992 *The Government's Expenditure Plans 1990–91 to 1992–93,* Cm 1021. chapter 21, page 38, and *Budget of the US Government FY 1991,* page 158, both using gdp deflators and financial years

Fig. 2

(Source: *Lloyds Bank Economic Bulletin,* no. 136, April 1990)

Table 1 DEFENCE AND THE UK ECONOMY

DOMESTIC ECONOMY	1989–90 £bn	% of UK total
Asset creation	5.8	6
Research and development	2.4	23
Other equipment, etc.	3.9	
Armed forces	5.8	
Civilian personnel	2.4	
Total, and % of gdp	20.3	4
	1987–88 £m	
Aerospace sales	2150	26
Electronics sales	1546	15

BALANCE OF PAYMENTS	1988 £m	
Visible		
Exports fob	781	1.0
Imports cif	264	0.3
Balance	+517	
Invisible		
Credits	293	0.3
Debits	2000	2.5
	–1707	
Total, and % of c/a deficit	–1190	8
Unidentified aerospace exports[1]	1300	1.6

REAL RESOURCES Manpower, and % of workforce	1989–90	
Full-time	000s	
Armed forces	321	1.2
Civilian personnel	141	0.5
Total	462	1.7
Part-time		
Reservists	323	1.2
Cadets	145	0.5
Defence-dependent jobs		
Direct	310	1.2
Indirect	255	0.9
Total	565	2.1
Land	m.ha.	% of total
Freehold	223	0.9
Leasehold and rights	116	0.5
Total	339	1.4
Energy	mtoe	
	3.2	1.5

1. Estimates from industry sources. No information is available on unidentified defence imports, so the unidentified exports have not been included in the balance of payments figures.
Sources: *The Government's Expenditure Plans 1990–91 to 1991–93,* chapters 1 and 21. Cm. 1001 and 1021. *Statement on the Defence Estimates 1989,* Cm. 675.

Study the two diagrams and the table on the impact of defence spending, and answer the following questions.

1 It is often argued that defence spending affects living standards by slowing economic growth.
   a Why should this be the case? (2)
   b Does the data in Figure 1 support this point of view? (3)

2 Using a production possibility curve diagram, show how the 'peace dividend' could help improve living standards. (4)

3 Using the information in Table 1, explain the economic effects of defence spending on the UK economy. (8)

4 Figure 2 shows what happened to defence spending in the UK and the USA in the period 1979–91.
   a What does the phrase 'real annual changes' mean? (2)
   b In what years did defence spending actually fall in the UK? (1)
   c What might explain the increase in defence spending in 1990–91? (1)
   d Outline the economic consequences of reducing defence spending. (4)

The effect of fiscal policy on the distribution of income

Redistribution of income through taxes and benefits, 1991

United Kingdom   £ per year

	Quintile groups of households ranked by equivalised disposable income[1]					
	Bottom fifth	Next fifth	Middle fifth	Next fifth	Top fifth	All households
Average per household (£ per year[1])						
Earnings of main earner	1 000	3 870	8 880	13 400	23 990	10 230
Earnings of others in the household	90	610	2 440	5 060	7 640	3 170
Occupational pensions, annuities	200	570	990	1 190	1 550	900
Investment income	180	420	740	1 170	3 630	1 230
Other income	100	180	250	290	400	240
Total original income	1 570	5 650	13 310	21 100	37 220	15 770
plus Benefits in cash						
Contributory	1 920	1 990	1 350	840	560	1 330
Non-contributory	1 970	1 530	970	530	330	1 060
Gross income	5 460	9 170	15 630	22 470	38 110	18 170
less Income tax[2] and NIC[3]	200	780	2 140	3 830	7 660	2 920
less Community charge[4] (gross)	540	580	660	680	660	620
Disposable income	4 730	7 820	12 830	17 960	29 790	14 620
less Indirect taxes	1 320	1 870	2 920	3 690	4 470	2 860
Post-tax income	3 410	5 940	9 900	14 270	25 320	11 770
plus Benefits in kind						
Education	1 090	900	1 190	890	560	920
National Health Service	1 480	1 410	1 280	1 120	940	1 250
Housing subsidy	140	120	50	30	10	70
Travel subsidies	50	50	50	60	90	60
School meals and welfare milk	70	30	20	10	10	30
Final income	6 230	8 450	12 500	16 380	26 910	14 090

1 Equivalised disposable income has been used for ranking the households into quintile groups
2 After tax relief at source on mortgage interest and life assurance premiums
3 Employees' national insurance contributions
4 Rates in Northern Ireland

(Source: Central Statistical Office, from the Family Expenditure Survey)

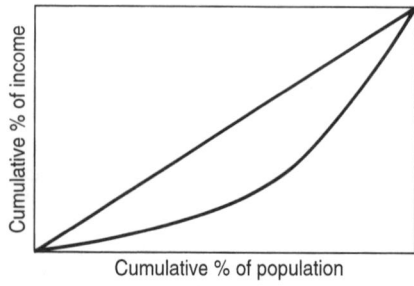

Cumulative % of income

Cumulative % of population   (Source: *Social Trends*, 1994)

Study the table and the diagram and answer the following questions.

1 a Using the data in the table, compare the distribution of original income with the distribution of final income. (4)
  b The diagram is called a Lorenz curve. What does the diagonal line show? (2)
  c The curve drawn on the diagram represents original income. Sketch the diagram and add a curve representing final income. (2)

2 a Give two examples of contributory benefits. (2)
  b What was the community charge replaced by? (1)
  c Why is education called a benefit in kind? (1)

3 a The UK has a progressive system of income tax. What does this mean? (2)
  b Does the data support the proposition that income tax in the UK is progressive? Explain and illustrate your answer. (4)
  c The standard rate of income tax in the UK is 25 per cent, plus national insurance contributions (NICs), yet the average tax paid is much less than this. Why? (3)

4 What factors might explain the distribution of NHS spending on the five income groups? (4)

5 List three factors which explain the inequality in the distribution of household income. (3)

The tax burden in the UK

Percentage of gross household income taken by direct and indirect taxation, 1979–91

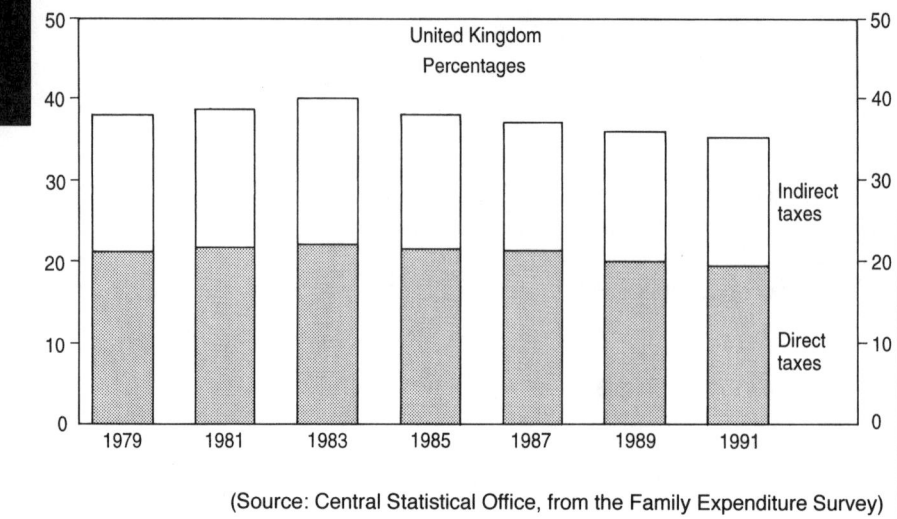

(Source: Central Statistical Office, from the Family Expenditure Survey)

Study the chart and answer the following questions.

1 a Give two examples of direct taxation. (2)
 b Give two examples of indirect taxation. (2)

2 One of the arguments against indirect taxes is that they tend to be regressive. Explain what this means and use a numerical example to explain your answer. (6)

3 a Using the data in the chart, explain what happened to the overall burden of taxation in the UK between 1979 and 1991. (3)
 b What changes occurred in the way taxes were raised after 1979? (3)

4 The Conservative government under John Major is committed to reducing the burden of direct taxation. What are the economic arguments for doing so? (4)

Health care – private or public?

Britain's health service is the most efficient in the world

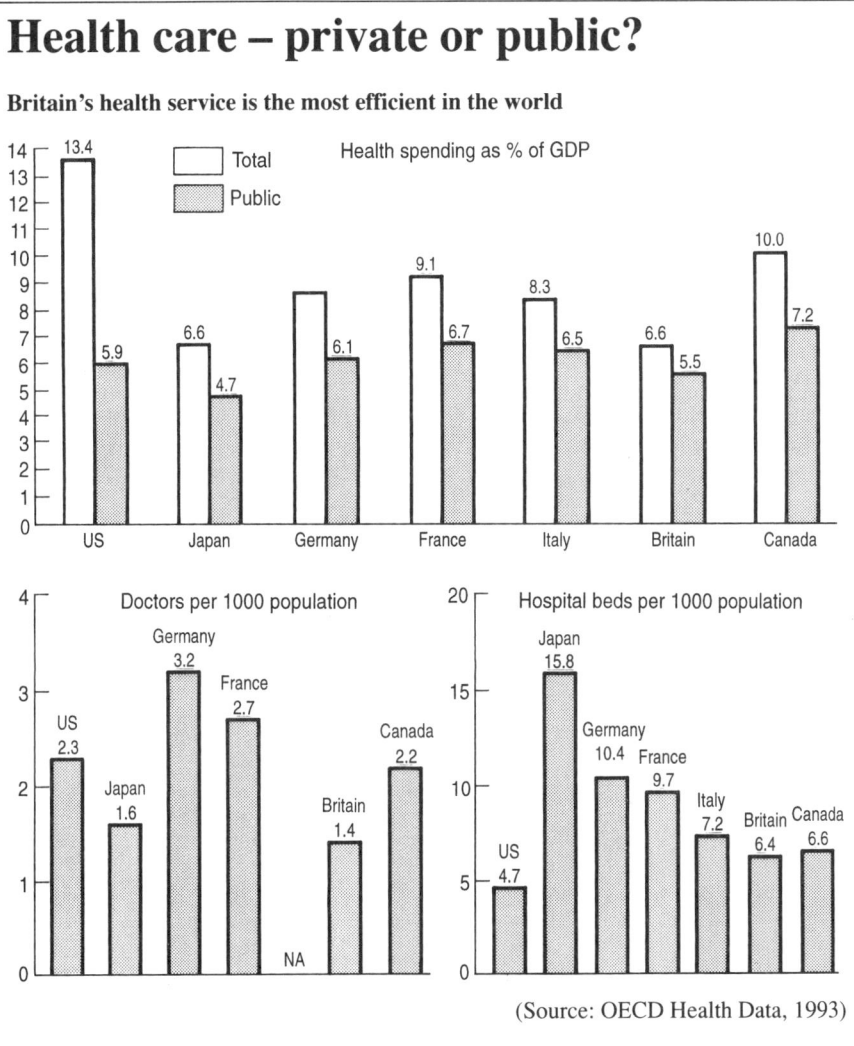

Health spending as % of GDP

(Source: OECD Health Data, 1993)

Study the information in the bar charts and then answer the following questions.

1 Use the data to describe the importance of the private and public sectors to medical provision in the seven countries analysed. (6)

2 Is it possible from the figures to determine which country spends most on health care? Explain your answer. (2)

3 Can the heading 'Britain's health service is the most efficient in the world' be justified? What other information would be helpful to support this statement? (9)

4 There are wide variations in the involvement of the government in health care provision between countries. Comment on the variations, and give reasons to support the view that health care should be provided by the public sector, not the free market. (8)

The impact of VAT on domestic energy

Extract from the Chancellor's Budget Speech March 1993

Two proposed measures will encourage the efficient use of fuel and reduce emissions of carbon dioxide and raise revenue. Together with measures already announced, these should achieve two-thirds of the UK target for reducing CO_2 emissions under the UN Convention on Climatic Change.

1 VAT will be charged on domestic fuel and power at 8% from 1 April 1994 and at the full standard rate from 1 April 1995. This will raise tax revenue of £950m in 1994/95 and £2300m in 1995/96.

2 Duty on petrol and other road fuels will be raised on average by at least 3% in real terms in future budgets following a rise of 10% proposed in this budget. This will raise an additional £195m from excise duty in 1993/94, £640m in 1994/95 and £1020m in 1995/96.

Table 1: *1991 Domestic Energy Expenditure by quintile groups of income*

Gross Normal weekly income of household

	Lowest 20%	2nd Quintile	3rd Quintile	4th Quintile	Highest 20%
Average Weekly Domestic Fuel Expenditure (£)	9.47	11.39	12.10	12.70	15.61
All Expenditure (£)	87.95	169.49	245.02	317.15	475.24

Table 2: *Household Income and Fuel Expenditure*

	Average Gross Weekly Household Income	Average Weekly Household Expenditure on Domestic Energy	Domestic Energy Expenditure as a % of Weekly Income
United Kingdom	£347.17	£11.68	3.4%
Northern Ireland	£273.95	£14.80	5.4%

(Source: 1991 Family Expenditure Survey)

Consider the extract from the chancellor's Budget speech and the two tables that follow.

1 a Using Table 1, calculate the importance of expenditure on fuel to each of the income groups. (5)
  b The fuel tax has been described as 'regressive'. What does this mean? (2)
  c Using the figures in Table 1, show whether or not this claim is justified. (3)

2 VAT on fuel has been set at 8 per cent as opposed to the standard rate of 17.5 per cent. Using the data in Table 2, compare the percentage of the average gross weekly income that would be paid by households in Northern Ireland with that in the UK as a whole. (4)

3 a Explain how the tax revenue from VAT on domestic energy was predicted to rise from £950 million in 1994/5 to £2300 million in 1995/6 even though the rate was only going to rise from 8 per cent to 17.5 per cent. (2)
b Using demand and supply diagrams, show why VAT on domestic energy should be so effective in raising tax revenue for the government. (5)

4 a Why is excise duty imposed on top of VAT? (1)
b What does it mean that duty on fuel will be raised by at least 3 per cent in real terms, and how is this likely to help the government achieve its environmental policy? (2)

5 One of the reasons given for imposing VAT on domestic fuel was that it would bring the UK into line with its partners in the European Union, who rely more heavily on expenditure taxes than Britain does. Describe some of the arguments for changing the burden of taxation from direct to indirect taxes. (6)

NICCEA, 1994, paper 3

How will we fill the £50 billion hole in our pocket?

The government is planning to borrow £50 billion this fiscal year (1993/4), £1 billion a week or nearly £1000 for every man, woman and child in the country. After allowing for the tax increases in the 1993 Spring Budget, that will fall to £44 billion in 1994/5, £39 billion in 1995/6, £33 billion in 1996/7 and to £30 billion in 1997/8. This level of borrowing is not sustainable.

Kenneth Clarke, the Chancellor, declared last week that he wants to be remembered for guiding British industry through a difficult period, and help 'in my own small way to make a difference to the wealth creating capacity of the nation', but he will fail if he does not take an axe to the budget deficit. In this he needs the full support of the Prime Minister, not the bland (and almost certainly incorrect) assurances that 70% of the deficit is due to the recession.

There are three priorities. The first, and most important, is to allow the economy to grow to its present potential, and to work at raising that potential. If the growth rate rose to 3.5% a year, borrowing would be cut to £10 billion or below, even without any further action on taxation and spending.

A second priority is tax reform. A model tax system was set out by Nigel Lawson in 1984. This would be one in which tax allowances and reliefs are abolished or severely restricted making room for sharply lower tax rates probably as low as 15% on personal taxation. Present allowances, reliefs and exemptions in Britain's tax system add up to an astonishing £14 billion a year.

A third priority is a radical agenda for public spending. The state's sole concern in welfare, for example, should be to provide a safety net through which the poorest should not be allowed to fall. Britain's blanket system of welfare fails that test. It doles out money to the middle classes, encourages welfare dependency among the poor and still leaves millions in squalor. In 1984 the Treasury, in a green paper on long term spending and taxation, said 'There is an inbuilt tendency for spending to rise, and an inbuilt resistance to expenditure reductions. Without firm control over public spending there can be no prospect of bringing the burden of tax back to tolerable levels.'

If these priorities are implemented they would eliminate the budget deficit, and turn the Tories into a tax-cutting party again.

(Adapted from *The Sunday Times*, 20 June 1993)

Consider the passage above, which relates to Britain's National Debt. Then answer the questions.

1 a What is meant by the National Debt? (2)
b According to the figures given in paragraph 1, by how much will the National Debt have increased by 1997/8? (2)

2 What does the author mean when he says in paragraph 1 that 'this level of borrowing is not sustainable'? (4)

3 In paragraph 2 the Prime Minister claims that 70 per cent of the budget deficit is due to the recession.
a Give four reasons why the budget deficit is likely to rise during a recession. (4)
b According to Keynes, how may this budget deficit help reduce the impact of a recession? (3)

4 a Using a diagram, distinguish between an economy growing to its present potential and raising that potential. (paragraph 3)   (4)
b Explain two actions which the government could take to help the economy grow to its potential.   (4)
c Explain three supply-side measures which may be implemented to raise the potential of the economy.   (6)

5 a What would you consider to be the characteristics of a 'good' tax?   (3)
b Given the criticisms levelled at the British tax system by the author in paragraph 4, why might many of the taxes in the UK be classed as 'bad' taxes?   (2)

6 a Give two examples of benefits which would be included in the 'blanket system of welfare' referred to in paragraph 5.   (2)
b What problems might the government encounter in getting 'firm control over public spending'?   (4)

NICCEA, 1994, paper 3

The European Union

Farmer earns £19,000 a year for growing nothing

For five years Bill Loyd has grown nothing on his 215 acres of high-quality arable land and in return for this inaction the Government pays him £19,000 a year. He is so pleased with this arrangement that he intends to sign a similar deal with the Ministry of Agriculture to cover the next five years.

Bill is one of 1,600 British farmers who have taken the European Union's set-aside policy as far as it could go and moved all their cropland out of production.

Set-aside was introduced six years ago as a means of reducing the European Community food mountains. Farmers could volunteer to stop growing crops in return for direct payments. Now it is central to the Common Agricultural Policy and the majority of British lowland arable farmers have been compelled to cease growing on at least 15 per cent of their acreage. This year, an area the size of Surrey is out of production and hundreds of farm workers have lost their jobs.

Whilst quite happy to accept £88 an acre for growing nothing, Bill Loyd is certain that set-aside is not a long-term solution to the problem of food surpluses. He agrees with the agriculture minister, Gillian Shepherd, that it is a 'Brussels fudge which must eventually collapse'.

Option that became almost compulsory

Set-aside has been transformed from an option into virtually a compulsory practice. Under the 1992 reform of the Common Agricultural Policy (CAP), European farmers have had to take 15 per cent of croplands out of production in order to get the subsidies they depend on.

The high guaranteed prices for cereals, which encouraged farmers to overproduce, are being rapidly lowered towards world market levels. By way of compensation, farmers are to receive direct payments for each acre planted with cereal crops plus a further payment for the area set aside. These support payments averaged £13,400 per English farm last year.

The fallow 15 per cent has to be shifted around the farm each year, so farmers cannot put only their least productive land into set-aside.

Farmers also have the option of earning £126 per acre by putting between 18 and 50 per cent of their land into long-term set-aside, with fields lying fallow for years on end. Farmers like Bill Loyd who set aside their entire arable acreage can grow nothing at all in return for £88 per acre.

(Source: Adapted from the *Independent*, 18 March 1994)

1 Using demand and supply diagrams, show how the 'high guaranteed prices' led to unsold food surpluses. (4)

2 Using demand and supply diagrams, show how set-aside could remove these surpluses. (4)

3 Describe two other policies that the European Union could use to remove these surpluses. (8)

4 Define **a** allocative efficiency and **b** technical efficiency. (4)

5 Does set-aside contribute to achieving allocative and technical efficiency? Explain your answer. (5)

6 Do you agree with the contention that set-aside must eventually collapse? Explain your answer. (5)

EC pays cinemas to show Eurofilms

British cinemas are being paid thousands of pounds in European Community subsidies to kick Hollywood blockbusters off their screens and replace them with European titles.

The scheme is part of a £160m system of grants that forms the little-known cinematic equivalent of the Common Agricultural Policy. It has already cost the British taxpayer £28m, and it is one reason why the Renoir cinema in London's West End is this weekend showing *Ma Saison Préférée* instead of *The Flintstones*.

Eight cinemas in London, Edinburgh, Glasgow and Belfast are paid up to £13,500 a year each by Brussels in return for showing a minimum 50% of European titles in their programmes. Another 100 cinemas will be added to the list in November. These grants are just the beginning. The whole programme, called Measures to Encourage the Development of European Audio-visual Industry (MEDIA), is earmarked for expansion with a proposed budget of £1 billion.

The idea of the programme is to form a bulwark against the 'cultural imperialism' of the Hollywood moguls. After four years, however, the pilot scheme has been a flop. American imports account for 80% of European viewing, while only one in five European films is seen in more than one community country.

The scheme has caused a split in the British Film establishment – with the old guard led by Lord Attenborough in favour of subsidy, while other directors and producers believe it fosters a loser's mentality.

A confidential audit of MEDIA reveals an alarming catalogue of abuse, waste and failure. The report reveals that:

- The Berlin-based European Film Academy spent 88% of its budget on overheads.
- Only 11% of the first 515 story ideas supported by the London-based European Script Fund went into production.
- A £2.3m-a-year project to dub films deliberately avoided using English, French or German and concentrated on Europe's minority languages.

(Source: Adapted from *The Sunday Times*, 31 July 1994)

Read the passage and then answer the following questions.

1 Explain, using an appropriate diagram, how EC grants can help promote European-made films. (4)

2 What economic and other arguments might be used to support the use of EC grants to subsidise European films? (6)

3 a According to economic theory, how does this kind of interference with markets affect the allocation of resources? (4)
b From the evidence contained in the article, has the use of grants improved efficiency in the European film industry? (4)

4 What other methods apart from grants might be used to protect the European film industry? (2)

Government intervention in agriculture

An argument in defence of government intervention in a particular sector of the economy is that the 'free market' does not provide the same incentives or rewards for the production of certain goods and services that society attaches to their production. In the case of UK agriculture, the problem has been largely one of low and unstable factor incomes in an industry responsible for providing a large part of the nation's food requirement.

Agriculture is generally regarded as suffering from an 'adjustment problem'. This relates to there being too many resources employed in the industry, with the result that factor incomes tend to be below those elsewhere in the economy. In addition, prices of agriculture are notoriously volatile. The biological nature of many of the production processes, and the importance of weather as a determinant of output, mean that market supplies are not totally within the control of the industry.

With demand for food being price inelastic, this random supply variability can cause severe price instability, with market prices typically 'see-sawing' from season to season. Such instability is often viewed as undesirable to both producers and consumers.

In most developed countries the principal objective of agricultural policy is income support, by which is meant the raising of factor incomes above their 'natural' market level. There is an inherent paradox here. Supporting incomes above market level retards the outflow of resources from the industry, thereby making worse the cause of the original problem.

Allied to the income support objective is that of price stability, with governments employing various methods to counter volatile markets.

Another justification for government intervention is frequently couched in terms of food security. Other markets have problems but are not singled out for special treatment, so why should agriculture be different? The answer lies, rightly or wrongly, in the desire to secure a domestic supply of food. The importance of this was highlighted by Britain's vulnerability as a large food importer during the second world war.

Another argument, more prevalent in the USA and continental Europe than in the UK, extols the virtues of a strong and healthy agricultural sector centred on the 'family farm'. Agriculture and the rural community are the backbone of society and worthy of protection.

These concerns have given rise to extensive government intervention in UK agriculture in the post-war period, initially under the 1947 Agricultural Act and, more recently, under the CAP of the European Union.

(Source: Adapted from the Northern Ireland Economic Council report, *The impact of CAP reform on Northern Ireland*, October 1993)

Read the passage and answer the following questions.

1 Give four objectives of government intervention in agricultural markets. (4)

2 Why might the free market underprovide certain goods and services, as suggested in paragraph 1? (3)

3 a How can a situation arise where too many resources are employed in an industry, even in cases where the free market is determining resource allocation? (3)

b How can government intervention (i) improve the working of the free market and (ii) reinforce the 'adjustment policy'? (4)

4 The article states that 'prices of agricultural outputs are notoriously volatile'. What does this mean and why does it happen? (6)

5 a What are positive externalities? (2)

b What positive externalities result from supporting agricultural production? (4)

c List four ways in which agriculture is supported through the Common Agricultural Policy. (4)

The effects of agricultural protection under CAP

Table 1 The Importance of Agriculture in the EU Budget, 1982–99

	1982	**1987**	**1992**	**1999***
Total EC Budget (m ECU)	20,706	35,783	61,097	84,098
Agricultural Expenditure (m ECU)	13,056	23,876	36,128	38,389
Agricultural Expenditure as % of Total EC Budget				

*Council of Ministers' forecast, in 1992 prices.

(Sources: Commission of the European Communities, *The Agricultural Situation in the Community*, annual reports; European Council of Ministers, *Conclusions of the Presidency*, December 1992)

Table 2 EU Self-Sufficiency* in Selected Commodities, 1989–91

Commodity	**Year**	**%**
Cereals	1989–90	120
Butter	1989	115
Skimmed Milk Powder	1989	145
Beef	1990	107
Sheep and Goat Meat	1990	81
Pigmeat	1990	104
Poultrymeat	1990	105
Sugar	1989–90	128
Wine	1990–91	103

*Self-sufficiency is the ratio of total EU production of the commodity to total EU consumption, expressed as a percentage.

(Source: Commission of the European Communities, *The Agricultural Situation in the Community*, annual reports)

Table 3 EU Internal and External Prices for Selected Commodities, 1986–88

Commodity	**Prices (ECU/tonne)**		
	Internal	**External**	**Ratio***
Soft Wheat	241	93	2.59
Barley	236	85	2.78
Maize	241	96	2.51
Hard Wheat	383	152	2.52
White Sugar	719	196	3.67
Skimmed Milk Powder	2,170	685	3.17
Butter	3,905	943	4.14
Beef	4,289	1,526	2.81

*The ratio of the EU market price to the world price   (Source: Agra Europe (1993))

Figure 1 CAP Price Support and Stabilisation

(Source: Northern Ireland Economic Council Report, 'The impact of CAP reform on Northern Ireland,' October 1993)

Study the tables and Figure 1. Then answer the following questions.

1 Using Table 1, calculate the percentage of the total EC budget devoted to agricultural support each year. (2)

2 a What is self-sufficiency (Table 2)? (1)
  b What is meant by a self-sufficiency ratio of 120? (1)
  c How does the information in Table 3 help explain the data in Table 2? (4)

3 a Using a demand and supply diagram, explain how the EC price for agricultural products is kept above the world price. (Figure 1 will help you with your answer.) (4)
  b During the 1993/94 GATT negotiations, the EC was heavily criticised for its agricultural policy by other producers of agricultural products. Using the information in Figure 1, explain why this should have been the case. (4)

4 a Does the data explain how European 'food mountains' arise? Explain your answer. (3)
  b Why might the EC have difficulty with the disposal of food mountains? (3)

5 How does EC intervention affect the allocative efficiency of resources within the agricultural sector of the European economy? (3)

Population

UK population structure

Age and sex structure of the population of the UK (percentages and millions)

Year	% of population under 16	% of population aged 16–39	% of population aged 40–64	% of population aged 65–79	% of population aged 80 and over	All ages (millions)
1991	**20.3**	**35.3**	**28.6**	**12**	**3.7**	**57.8**
Male	21.4	36.7	29	10.6	2.3	28.2
Female	19.3	34	28.2	13.3	5.2	29.6
2031	**18.4**	**28.7**	**30.3**	**15.6**	**6.9**	**62.1**
Male	19	29.7	30.9	14.9	5.5	30.7
Female	17.7	27.8	29.8	16.4	8.3	31.4

(Source: Adapted from *Social Trends*, 1992)

Study the table and answer the questions below.

1 What are the main changes expected to occur in the population structure of the UK between the years 1991 and 2031? (6)

2 From the information given in the table, do males or females have the longer life expectancy? Explain your answer. (4)

3 Calculate **a** the number of people under 16 and **b** the number of people over 65 in 1991 and in 2031. (4)

4 What are the implications of the trends shown in the data for **a** the government, **b** the transport industry, **c** the construction industry and **d** the leisure industry? (8)

5 a What is meant by the dependent population? (1)
b Suggest two changes which would alter the size of the dependent population. (2)

Marriage break-up in the UK

Divorce: by duration of marriage

United Kingdom — Percentages and thousands

	Year of divorce			
	1961	**1971**	**1981**	**1991**
Duration of marriage (percentages)				
0–2 years	1.2	1.2	1.5	9.3
3–4 years	10.1	12.2	19.0	14.0
5–9 years	30.6	30.5	29.1	27.0
10–14 years	22.9	19.4	19.6	18.3
15–19 years	} 13.9	{ 12.6	12.8	12.8
20–24 years		{ 9.5	8.6	9.5
25–29 years	} 21.2	{ 5.8	4.9	5.0
30 years and over		{ 8.9	4.5	4.1
All durations (=100%) (thousands)	27.0	79.2	155.6	171.1

(Source: Office of Population Censuses and Surveys; General Register Office Scotland)

Study the data and answer the questions below.

1 a From the data given in the table, describe the trends in divorce patterns in the UK between 1961 and 1991. (6)
b From the information provided, is it possible to calculate the divorce rate for the UK? Explain your answer. (2)

2 What are the economic implications of the trends in divorce between 1961 and 1991? (6)

3 a What does the economist mean by 'social costs'? (2)
b What are the social costs of a rising divorce rate? (4)

Answers to the exercises

1 UK export index, 1983–92 (1985 = 100)

Year	Export index
1983	77.8
1984	90.1
1985	100
1986	93.1
1987	101.5
1988	103
1989	118.2
1990	130.4
1991	132.6
1992	137.3

2 UK export index, 1983–92 (1990 = 100)

Year	Export index
1983	59.7
1984	69.1
1985	76.7
1986	71.4
1987	77.8
1988	79.0
1989	90.6
1990	100
1991	101.7
1992	105.2

3 UK soft drinks consumption index, 1985–92 (1990 = 100)

Year	Expenditure index
1985	53.1
1986	61.4
1987	69.5
1988	78.1
1989	88.7
1990	100
1991	105.1
1992	109.5

4 The set of data shown in Table 3 has been deflated to eliminate inflation. This is achieved by measuring the consumption of soft drinks throughout the entire period at the drinks prices which existed in 1990. The calculation required is to take the actual expenditure on drinks in any year, multiply by the price of drinks in 1990 and divide by the price of the current year. This gives us *real* consumer expenditure on soft drinks, which we can see increased steadily between 1985 and 1992. It remained virtually unchanged between 1991 and 1992, probably because of the recession.

Table 2 shows a constant increase in expenditure on soft drinks, but does not tell us how much of the increase is attributable to an increase in the number of units purchased and how much to increased prices per unit.

5   This question involves a slight variation on the usual theme of asking you to use RPI figures to calculate the real value of a variable. In this case you are given the value of soft drinks expenditure measured both in money and real terms. From this you are asked to calculate the RPI figure which was used to calculate the real value of soft drinks expenditure.
    The method used is as follows:

$$\text{actual expenditure} \times \frac{\text{RPI 1990}}{\text{RPI current year}}$$
$$= \text{real expenditure at constant 1990 prices}$$

Using the figures for 1985, we get:

$$1697 \times \frac{100}{\text{RPI 1985}} = 2199$$

We can now rearrange this equation to obtain the value of the RPI in 1985:

$$\text{RPI 1985} = \frac{1697 \times 100}{2199}$$
$$= 77.2$$

The figures for the other years are as follows.

Year	RPI
1986	75.7
1987	77.5
1988	87.5
1989	91.6
1990	100
1991	104.3
1992	108.2

6   a The base year is 1985.
    b

Year	Output (% change)
1982	+8
1983	−5.3
1984	+16.7
1985	−4.8
1986	−2
1987	+1
1988	−2
1989	+1

7 This requires the use of the simple formula for the calculation of index numbers.

$$\frac{\text{current figure}}{\text{base year figure}} \times 100$$

To calculate the figure for 1981:

$$\frac{\text{1981 figure}}{\text{1985 figure}} \times 100 = 88$$

Since we know that the 1985 figure is £5553 million, then the 1981 figure must be 88 per cent of this, which is £4886.6 million. The other figures are:

Year	Output (£m)
1982	5275.4
1983	4997.7
1984	5830.7
1985	5553
1986	5441.9
1987	5497.5
1988	5386.4
1989	5441.9

8 **a**

(i)

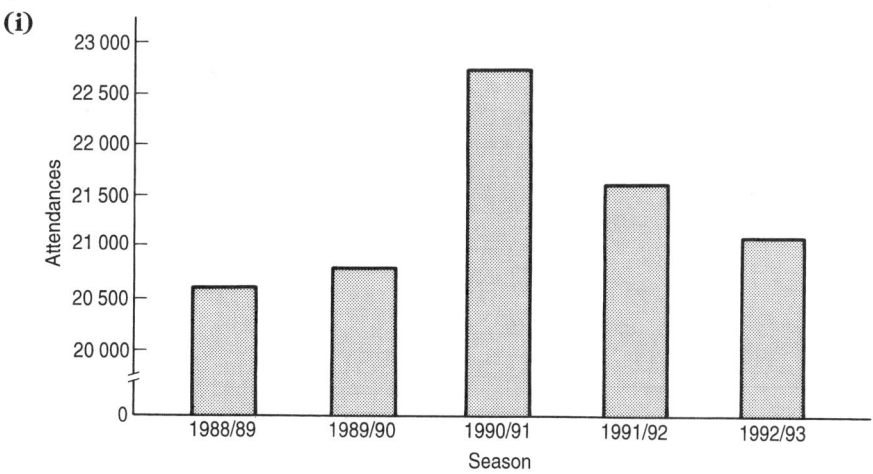

(ii)

Season	Attendance index
1988/89	100
1989/90	101
1990/91	110.1
1991/92	105
1992/93	102.5

b Two economic factors which might have contributed to the decline in attendances are (i) the recession with its associated rise in unemployment and fall in disposable income, and (ii) a rise in admission charges to Premier League games.

9 a

Summer 1990	+5%
Autumn 1990	+4.8%
Winter 1990	+9.1%
Spring 1991	no change
Summer 1991	−8.3%
Autumn 1991	+4.5%
Winter 1991	+4.3%

b To get the seasonally adjusted change we must remove that part of the actual change that has been caused by purely seasonal factors. Paradoxically, this may require us to add to the actual change rather than reduce it. For instance, in the summer of 1990 unemployment rose when seasonal factors would normally have caused it to fall. Hence the seasonally adjusted change was

$$5\% + 2.2\% = 7.2\%$$

However, in the autumn of that year unemployment rose by 4.8 per cent but 1.5 per cent of this was due to seasonal factors and so we deduct this to get a seasonally adjusted change of

$$4.8\% - 1.5\% = 3.3\%$$

The remaining figures are as follows.

Winter 1990	$9.1\% - 2.5\% = +6.6\%$
Spring 1991	$0 + 1.8\% = +1.8\%$
Summer 1991	$-8.3\% + 2.2\% = -6.1\%$
Autumn 1991	$4.5\% - 1.5\% = +3.0\%$
Winter 1991	$4.3\% - 2.5\% = +1.8\%$

10 a

$$1984 \quad £10 \times \frac{94.3}{89.8} = £10.50$$

$$1985 \quad £10 \times \frac{100}{89.8} = £11.14$$

$$1986 \quad £10 \times \frac{103.4}{89.8} = £11.51$$

$$1987 \quad £10 \times \frac{107.7}{89.8} = £11.99$$

$$1988 \quad £10 \times \frac{113.0}{89.8} = £12.58$$

b

$$1986 \quad £10 \times \frac{103.4}{100} = £10.34$$

$$1987 \quad £10 \times \frac{107.7}{100} = £10.77$$

$$1988 \quad £10 \times \frac{113.0}{100} = £11.30$$

11 a The real value in 1984 $= £10 \times \dfrac{89.8}{94.3} = £9.52$

b The real value in 1985 $= £10 \times \dfrac{89.8}{100} = £8.98$

c The real value in 1986 $= \pounds 10 \times \dfrac{89.8}{103.4} = \pounds 8.68$

d The real value in 1987 $= \pounds 10 \times \dfrac{89.8}{107.7} = \pounds 8.34$

e The real value in 1988 $= \pounds 10 \times \dfrac{89.8}{113} = \pounds 7.95$

12 a

(i)   Percentage change in quantity demanded $= 10\%$
Percentage change in price $= 50\%$
Price elasticity of demand $= 0.2$

(ii) Percentage change in quantity demanded $= \dfrac{1000}{9000} \times 100 = 11.1\%$

Percentage change in price $= \dfrac{100}{300} \times 100 = 33.3\%$

Price elasticity of demand $= 0.33$

b Percentages are not the same in reverse. When the price rose from £200 to £300 this was a 50 per cent rise, but when it fell from £300 to £200, this was a fall of 33.3%. Similarly with sales, a fall from 10 000 to 9000 is 10 per cent, but a rise from 9000 to 10 000 is 11.1%.

13 a

(i)   Percentage change in demand $= +100\%$
Percentage change in income $= +25\%$
Income elasticity of demand $= 4$
This is an income elastic item as the figure is greater than 1.
(ii) Percentage change in demand for Grotto $= -40\%$
Percentage change in income $= +25\%$
Income elasticity of demand $= -1.6$

b The minus sign tells us that Grotto lager is an inferior good. Families normally buy less of it as their standard of living improves. It is only purchased because better quality beer is not affordable and when this situation changes consumers move 'up market' and abandon Grotto.

14 a *Wimbledon*: Between 1981 and 1993 the attendance rose from 358 000 to 393 000, a rise of 9.8 per cent.
The Grand National: Here attendance fell from 56 000 in 1981 to 50 000 in 1993, a fall of 10.7 per cent.
The Derby: This event experienced the most spectacular fall in attendance, down from 50 000 in 1981 to 27 000 in 1993. This represents a drop of 46 per cent.
The Varsity rugby match: This was the largest overall gainer, with attendance up from 28 000 in 1981 to 66 000 in 1993. This is a rise of 135.7%.
The Open golf championship: This was the most volatile performer with a consistent trend hard to identify. Between 1981 and 1986 attendance rose by 19.6 per cent and between then and 1991 it rose by a further 43 per cent. However, between 1991 and 1993 it fell by 27.1 per cent. Over the entire period attendance rose by 25 per cent.

b Highest percentage increase – Varsity rugby match.
Highest percentage decrease – the Derby.

UK trade union membership index,
1981–91 (1981 = 100)

Year	TU membership index
1981	100
1982	95.9
1983	92.6
1984	90.9
1985	89.3
1986	86.8
1987	86.8
1988	86.0
1989	84.3
1990	81.8
1991	79.3

The index of trade union membership fell from a base of 100 in 1981 to 79.3 in 1991. The percentage fall is

$$\frac{100 - 79.3}{100} = 20.7\%$$

b In 1981, the 12.1 million trade unionists represented 50.4 per cent of civilian workers. Hence the total number of civilian workers must have been

$$\frac{12.1 \times 100}{50.4} = 24 \text{ million}$$

The figures for the other years are:

Year	Civilian workforce (millions)
1982	23.6
1983	23.2
1984	24.2
1985	24.3
1986	24.4
1987	25.4
1988	26.1
1989	26.8
1990	26.3
1991	25.5

Index

absolute amount of public spending 52-53
accelerator theory 102
accounts, balancing 44
ad valorem tax 62
aggregate demand and supply 53, 61
allocative efficiency 67, 93, 132, 137
An Enquiry into the Nature and Causes of the Wealth of Nations 58
Annual Abstract of Statistics 4
Annual Report of the National Food Survey Committee (1987) 4
arithmetic mean 8
Attlee, Clement 56
automatic stabiliser 53, 64
average rate of taxation 59
averages 5, 8-9
averages, weighted 8-9, 12

balance of invisibles 42
balance of payments 39, 45-6, 57, 115, 116, 120
balance of payments deficit 43
balance of trade 39, 119
  recent trends in 40
balance of trade deficit 39
balancing item 44-5
Bank of England 109-10
  interest rates and 49
  intervention buying and 48-9, 118
Barclay's Bank Economic Review 4
base date 10
base rate 112-13
base year 6-7
'basket' of currencies 12-13, 50
Belfast News Letter 108
Beveridge, Lord 57
Beveridge Report (1944) 34, 56
black economy 34, 108
Black Wednesday 50, 118
Blue Book 3, 14, 41
Bretton Woods Conference (1944) 48
budget deficit 53, 65-6, 130

capital flows 43
capital gains tax liability 28
Care in the Community 55
central government 52
Central Statistical Office 16, 44, 126
ceteris paribus 18-19, 48
changes in official reserves 44
civil aviation 40
Clarke, Kenneth 65, 111, 130
Common Agricultural Policy (CAP) 132, 134, 135
  agricultural protection under 136-7

community charge or 'poll tax' 59, 124, 125
comparative advantage 121
competitiveness
  in book publishing 90
  in cross-Channel market 88-9
  improving Britain's 117
  Japanese responses to changed 51
  in Ulster 103-4
composition of public spending 53-5
concentration ratio 90
Confederation of British Industry (CBI) 112
congestion tax 70
Conservative government, home owners and 65
consumer confidence 100-1, 112-13
consumption function 18
corporation tax 61
cost of living index 15, 27-9
cost of tax collection 62
cross-elasticity of demand 17, 87
cross-sectional data 76-7
crowding out 55, 65
current account balance 42-3

Daily Telegraph, The 109
data 3
  analysing the 5, 78
  approaching different types of 75-8
  index number form 6, 7-8
  presentation of 3
  seasonally adjusted 16
  sources of 3-4
defence, public spending on 54, 117, 122-3
demand curve, an inverse relationship 16
demand and supply analysis 15, 47, 82, 84
de-merit goods 68, 83
demographic trends 54-5
deposits and lending by UK residents, other than banks and government 44
depreciation 48, 94
direct investment 44
direct relationships of variables 17-18
direct taxes 60-1, 126

economic forecasting 18, 111
economic growth 65-6, 130-1
  defence spending and 123
  exports and 94-5
  rate in UK 53
  social security and 55
  supply-side measures and 117
economic theory
  importance of 77-8
  interference with markets and 133

149

Economic Trends 4
economic variables
  cross-sectional data and 76-7
  inflation and 13
  relationships between 5, 16-19
  time-series data and 75
Economist, The 4
education
  merit goods 68, 125
  public spending and 54
efficiency 93
environmental policies 69-70, 80
European Community (EC) grants 133
European Union (EU) 42
  exchange rate mechanism and 48
  set-aside policy 132
  Social Chapter 71
  tax harmonisation 61, 129
  UK trade and 39
exchange rate mechanism (ERM) 48, 51
  Britain's departure from 49-50, 118
exchange rates
  determinants of 47
  economic effects of movements in 47-8
  government intervention 48-9
  international trade and 112
external assets 43
external assets and liabilities, transactions in 43-4
externalities
  markets and 68-9, 135
  negative, government response to 69
external liabilities 43

Family Expenditure Survey 4, 9, 27, 126
financial and other services 41
Financial Times, The 4, 33, 37-8, 51, 84, 96, 99, 119, 121
fiscal policy 57, 94-5, 124
fixed exchange rates 48
foreign investment, types of 44
free market economics 34, 79, 83
free market economies
  achievements of 67, 79
  health care and 127
  underprovision of goods and services 67-8, 134
Friedman, Professor Milton 83

GDP 14, 99
  components of UK 102
  impact of nationalisation on 56
  PSBR as percentage of 64
  public spending as percentage of 55-7
  real 53
GDP deflator 14
General Agreement on Tariffs and Trade (GATT) 137

general government 41, 63
  expenditure as percentage of GDP 56
George, Eddie 111
government intervention
  agriculture and 134-5
  environmental problems and 69-70, 80
  exchange rates and 48-9
Greater London, unemployment rate (1993) 37
gross national product (GNP) 72
Guardian, The 4

headline inflation 30
health
  example of merit good 68
  public spending on 54-5, 127
HMSO *Financial Statement and Budget Report* (1989/90) 4

incentives to save, indirect taxes and 62
income effect, taxes and 61-2
income elasticity of demand 22, 77-8
independent central bank 111
Independent, The 4, 132
indexation tables 28
index-linked gilts 28
index-linked pensions 28
index-linking 15, 28
index number form 6
  converting data into 7-8
index numbers 5, 7-8
indirect taxes 60-1, 126
  effect on demand 62
  effects of shift towards 61
  incentives to save and 62
  reasons for change to 61-2
inequality, markets and 71
inflation 27-8, 57, 108, 109-10
  alternative measures of 29-30
  calculating the rate of 6
  government borrowing and 65
  index-linking and 15
  post-war trends in 30-1
  rates in UK (1980-89) 32
  underlying 30
Inland Revenue, the 28, 44, 60
interest, profits and dividends 41
interest rate
  Bank of England and 49
  inversely related to employment 16
  real rate 13, 108
International Labour Organisation 34
International Monetary Fund (IMF) 64, 79
international trade, exchange rates and 112
intervention buying, Bank of England and 48
invalidity benefit 55

inverse relationship of variables
  demand curve 16
  Phillips curve 17
investment 98
  accelerator theory 102
  types of foreign 44, 114-15
'invisible hand' 67
invisible trade 40-3

Keynesian analysis 17, 71-2, 95, 99
Keynes, J.M. 57, 64, 66, 130

Laffer curve 62
Lamont, Norman 118
'Lawson boom' 35, 40, 43, 53, 64
Lawson, Nigel 31, 53, 66, 130
lending to overseas residents by UK banks 44
Lilley, Peter 55
local authority, direct taxes and 60
local government 52
Lorenz curve 124-5

Maastricht agreement 51
Mail on Sunday, The 91
Major, John 65, 98, 126
marginal rate of tax 59
market failure 67
  areas of 57, 67-71
  taxes to correct 58
markets, inequalities and 71-2
market system, versus planned system 79
Marshall-Lerner condition 48
Measures to Encourage the
  Development of European Audio-visual
  Industry (MEDIA) 133
median, calculating the 8
merit goods 56, 67-8
minimum wage debate 71
mode, calculating the 8
monetarism, inflation and 31, 65, 111
monetary terms 13
money values, real values and 13-14
monopolies, development of 70-1, 93
Monopolies and Mergers Commission 71

national debt, inflation and 65, 130
National Insurance 29, 125
nationalised industries 56-7
NATO 42
natural monopolies 28, 70-1
negative externalities
  government response to 69
  indirect taxation and 62
negative income elasticity, 77-8
Nesbitt, R.C. 37
non-price factors 48
North America, UK exports to 39, 119

Observer, The 90
OECD countries 117
OECD Financial Statistics (1992) 4, 19
Office of Fair Trading (OFT) 91
oligopolies 70, 89

peace dividend 54, 122-3
pensioner price index 29
pensions, index-linking of 15
percentages 5-6
Phillips curve 17, 19, 34, 71, 110
Pink Book 3, 39, 44
pollution
  government response to 69-70
  increasing taxes on fuel and 62
  taxes on petrol 58
population
  elderly as proportion of UK (1991-2031)
    55
  structure of UK 138
portfolio investment 44
price elasticity of demand 22, 48, 62, 85, 91,
  112, 121
price inelasticity, demand for food and 134
pricing policies of public utilities 28
privatisation
  British Rail and 93
  major companies and 57
  prisons and 54
producer price index (PPI) 29
profit margin 6, 69
progressive tax 58, 125
proportional taxes 59
public corporations 52
public expenditure 52-5, 131
  absolute amount of 52
  composition of 52, 53-5
  as percentage of GDP 52, 55-7
public finance 52
public good 67, 80
public order, spending on 54
public sector 52
  health care in 127
public sector borrowing requirement (PSBR)
  63-5, 96-7, 108
  history of 64-5
  interest rates and 56
  size of 64
  views about 65
public sector debt repayment (PSDR) 65
public services, spending on 54
purchasing power parity (PPP) 117

quantity theory of money 108

'real' economic variable, inflation and 38
real gains 28

real values
    calculating 13
    money values and 5, 13-14
recession 31, 35, 40, 55, 57, 64, 103-4
Red Book 3
redistribution of income 57
    controversy over 71
    taxes and state benefits UK (1991) 59, 124
Regional Trends 4, 107
regressive taxes 59-60, 126, 128
relationships between economic
    variables 5, 16-19
        direct 17-18
        identifying 77
        inverse 16-17
retail price index (RPI)
    base date and 10
    base year figure and 6
    calculating changes in 10
    compiling 27-8
    uses of 13, 28
    weighted average and 5, 9

savings ratio 98, 99, 101
seasonal adjustments, GDP and 99
seasonally adjusted data 5, 16
sea transport 40, 116
services 40
    civil aviation 40
    financial and other 41
    general government expenditure 41
    sea transport 40
Sheehy Report (1993) 54
simple average, calculating the 8
single European currency 50, 51
Smith, Adam 58, 67
social costs
    drugs and 83
    marriage break-up and 139
    pollution and 69
social security, government spending and 55
Social Trends 3, 4, 60, 92-3, 124, 138
social welfare benefits 28, 53, 57
    blanket system of 66, 131
Soros, George 50
specific tax, effect of 62
state earnings related pension scheme
    (SERPS) 55
sterling, decline of 50-1, 118
sterling index 13
sterling trade weighted index 5, 12-13, 50
substitution effect, taxes and 61-2
Sunday Times, The 4, 66, 86, 88, 105, 111,
    112, 130, 133
supply curve 17, 49

effect of specific tax 62
supply-side policies 35, 59, 61, 71-2, 104,
    117, 131

taxation
    direct and indirect 60-3
    government spending and 122-31
    principles of 58
    progressive 58-9, 125
    proportional 59
    reasons for 57-8, 63
    regressive 59-60
    UK burden of 126
tax exempt special saving accounts (TESSAs)
    62
tax and prices index (TPI) 29-30
tax reform 66
Thatcher, Margaret 31, 34, 57, 65, 109, 118
time lags 18, 77
time-series data 75-6
Times, The 4, 85
trade, geographical analysis of 39
trade union membership in UK (1981-91)
    23, 148
trade unions, wage claims and 32
transactions, external assets and liabilities
    and 43-4
transfers 42, 46
transmission mechanism, variables and 17
travel 41
types of visible trade 39

UK balance of trade deficit (1989) 32
underlying inflation 30
unemployment 53, 57, 105-7
    counter-inflationary policies and 31
    criteria for 33
    post-war trends in 34-5
    presenting the figures 34
    regional distribution of 36-8, 107
    seasonal adjustments to 16
    UK (1980-90) 76
United Nations Convention on Climatic
    Change 128
United Nations (UN) 42

VAT
    EU tax harmonisation and 61, 129
    goods and services 60-1
    impact on domestic energy 59-61, 128
visible trade 39, 119-20

wages councils, abolition of 35
weighted averages 8-9, 12
working population 34